W9-CBP-859

Church
in the
Present Tense

Emergent Village resources for communities of faith

An Emergent Manifesto of Hope
edited by Doug Pagitt and Tony Jones

Organic Community
Joseph R. Myers

Signs of Emergence
Kester Brewin

Justice in the Burbs
Will and Lisa Samson

Intuitive Leadership
Tim Keel

The Great Emergence
Phyllis Tickle

Make Poverty Personal
Ash Barker

Free for All
Tim Conder and Daniel Rhodes

The Justice Project
Brian McLaren, Elisa Padilla, and Ashley Bunting Seeber, eds.

Thy Kingdom Connected
Dwight Friesen

Formational Children's Ministry
Ivy Beckwith

www.emersionbooks.com

Church
in the
Present Tense

A Candid Look at
What's Emerging

Scot McKnight, Peter Rollins, Kevin Corcoran, Jason Clark

BrazosPress

a division of Baker Publishing Group
Grand Rapids, Michigan

Published by Brazos Press
a division of Baker Publishing Group
P.O. Box 6287, Grand Rapids, MI 49516-6287
www.brazospress.com

Printed in the United States of America

ISBN 978-1-58743-299-6

Unless otherwise indicated, Scripture quotations are from the New Revised Standard Version of the Bible, copyright © 1989, by the Division of Christian Education of the National Council of the Churches of Christ in the United States of America. Used by permission. All rights reserved.

Scripture quotations marked NIV are from the HOLY BIBLE, NEW INTERNATIONAL VERSION®. NIV®. Copyright © 1973, 1978, 1984 by International Bible Society. Used by permission of Zondervan. All rights reserved.

Scripture quotations marked RSV are from the Revised Standard Version of the Bible, copyright 1952 [2nd edition, 1971] by the Division of Christian Education of the National Council of the Churches of Christ in the United States of America. Used by permission. All rights reserved.

11   12   13   14   15   16   17   7   6   5   4   3   2   1

In keeping with biblical principles of creation stewardship, Baker Publishing Group advocates the responsible use of our natural resources. As a member of the Green Press Initiative, our company uses recycled paper when possible. The text paper of this book is comprised of 30% post-consumer waste.

ēmersion is a partnership between Baker Publishing Group and Emergent Village, a growing, generative friendship among missional Christians seeking to love our world in the Spirit of Jesus Christ. The ēmersion line is intended for professional and lay leaders like you who are meeting the challenges of a changing culture with vision and hope for the future. These books will encourage you and your community to live into God's kingdom here and now.

Emergent Village resources for communities of faith

Contents

Acknowledgments

I wish to thank the following individuals and institution for support and encouragement during various stages of this project: Jonny Baker; Kester Brewin; Allistair Duncan; Brian McLaren; Archbishop Rowan Williams; each of the other authors: Scot, Peter, and Jason; Bob Hosack and Jeremy Cunningham of Brazos Press; Kurt and Lori Wilson for friendship and for their many tangible contributions to this book and the courses out of which it grew; and John Witvliet and the Institute for Christian Worship at Calvin College. The Institute made it possible not only to include the very talented team of Kurt and Lori Wilson on this project but also to collaborate with students in ways meaningful not only to them but to me as well. Thanks to all of you.

Introduction

The Emerging Church

KEVIN CORCORAN

The Christian church has a history. The birth of the church traces its lineage back to Jesus from Nazareth, and more specifically to a community's belief in the incarnation, life, death, and resurrection of Jesus as the Christ. Of course, the Christ event itself is embedded in a history, a peculiarly *Jewish* history. Absent that (Jewish) history, the Christ event is evacuated of theological significance. That a human being should rise from the dead would certainly be a historical curiosity, just another startling oddity in a world that throws up such natural oddities as carnivorous plants and marsupial wolves. But absent a narrative of sin and redemption, a narrative of kingship and exodus, a resurrection from the dead would remain nothing more than an odd curiosity.

What we know as the *emerging church* is no different. It too has a history. Its history begins in the early 1990s in the United Kingdom. It was there, in London, that people like Jonny Baker (who appears on the DVD insert that accompanies this volume), Ian Mobsby, and others began what can best be described as *experiments in worship*. These communities were self-consciously contextual, both culturally and geographically. The aesthetics of their worship reflected the gifts, skills, and talents of the human resources indigenous to its members, which included artists of various sorts, writers, social visionaries, and the like. These communities also exploited the emerging cultural resources known and daily used by its members, including technological resources such as new media and social networking resources that were just coming into existence via the world wide web.

Many of these experiments were not originally undertaken outside or in opposition to the institutional church, which in the United Kingdom is the Anglican Church. Often these experimental groups began within and with the aid and blessing of the Anglican Church. Today the archbishop of Canterbury and leader of the worldwide Anglican Communion, Rowan Williams, is a staunch defender of the movement. (An interview with the archbishop is included on the DVD accompanying this volume.) "Fresh expressions" is the phrase currently being employed to describe these new ways of doing church within Anglicanism. The term *emerging*, which is also used in the United Kingdom, is actually a fairly recent American export.

What we know as the emerging church in the United States began later, in the late 1990s. And unlike the *alternative worship* movement in the United Kingdom, it seems fair to say that the US emerging church movement began as a reaction against institutional church within evangelical Protestantism. Emergent Village, for example, originally began as a small band of disillusioned friends who gathered for the purpose of forging a way to follow Jesus at the end of the twentieth century and at the dawn of the twenty-first.

In 2000 Tony Jones met with friends in the Minnesota woods to dream about, argue about, and contemplate the future of Christianity. A year later Brian McLaren, Doug Pagitt, Tim Keel, and others adopted the "emerging" moniker. Since then, and thanks in no small measure to the explosion of Internet blogs and new means of social networking, the emerging church has been spreading like a virus.

It seems fair to say that while the alternative worship movement in the United Kingdom was, at the beginning, primarily concerned with rethinking and reimagining worship practices, the emerging church in the United States was from its inception concerned with rethinking and reimagining Christian theology as well as Christian practice.

Despite these differences the emerging church in the United States and its British counterpart share the same animating principles and ethos. Below I describe the emerging church as it exists today on both sides of the Atlantic.

The Church and Postmodernism

Each January I teach a three-week course in London and Belfast on the emerging church. To give you a feel for an emerging church, let me describe an experience I had several years ago in London. I was participating in an Anglo-Catholic Mass in a very old church that blended ancient ritual, liturgy, and creeds with the use of the latest image and sound reproduction, including an elegant MacBook Pro, which was perched on the altar table just to the left of the consecrated elements. I found this juxtaposition utterly shocking. There was the priest, dressed in high-church vestments and performing the liturgy, ancient and regal. And also there—a MacBook Pro. On the altar!

What to me seemed initially incongruous was to my students ho hum. Bread and wine are ordinary things; so too a laptop computer. If the former can become for us the body and blood of Christ, why can't the other, ordinary though it may be, function as a window through which God's love and mercy are communicated via image and sound?

Postmodernism, as I point out in "Who's Afraid of Philosophical Realism?" is both a *cultural* phenomenon and a *philosophical* movement. Cultural postmodernism involves various and sundry sorts of cultural shifts, sensibilities, and notions, while philosophical postmodernism involves, among other things, calling into question "metanarratives," or grand stories of the world and our place in it. The Christian story is one such narrative. Atheistic naturalism is another. Consciously or not, each of us fits our own particular story into a larger story (or stories). What gets called into question by philosophical postmodernism is our ability to float free of the grand narratives we find ourselves in and to view things from a "God's eye view." Those sensitive to the postmodern situation, like those in the emerging and altworship movements, claim that our grasp of reality is always partial, incomplete, fragmentary. This, I suggest, leads those in the movement to emphatically promote tolerance and enthusiastically participate in dialogue—religious, political, and otherwise.

Second, emerging Christians tend to be theologically pluralistic and suspicious of tidy theological boxes. They believe that God is bigger than any theology and that God is first and foremost a storyteller, not a dispenser of theological doctrine and factoids. Theology for them, therefore, is conceived as an ongoing and provisional conversation. Indeed, many prefer the descriptor "emerging conversation" to "emerging church."

Emerging Christians are also allergic to thinking that fixates on who is going to heaven and who is going to hell, or on who's on the inside and who's on the outside. They stress the importance of right living (ortho*praxy*) over right believing (ortho*doxy*). What's important, some often say, is whether you engage in God-love and neighbor-love. They believe the gospel is a radically *this-worldly* bit of good news.

Third, emerging Christians believe the church must change if it is to speak meaningfully to a postmodern culture. So, like the prophet Amos, the rhetoric of emerging Christians can be shocking, alarming, and hyperbolic. They are frequently given to dramatic overstatement. But it should be kept in mind that, at its best and most sincere, the aim of the rhetoric is to rouse us (the church) from dogmatic slumber, to get us to see old things with new eyes, or sometimes to see completely new things. The aim, one might say, is to unsettle us such that a space is open for God to break in and to speak afresh, and then for us to get on with God's agenda in the world. At its worst, however, the rhetoric of emerging Christians can be sloppy, unnecessarily misleading, obnoxiously jargon laden, and incoherent.

Fourth, participants in the emerging and altworship movements are passionate about the present. The gospel, they want us to realize, is about the here and now and not a ticket to secure a place in the there and then of heaven. This passion for the present manifests itself in four overlapping foci: community, transformation, worship, and social engagement.

Community

Emerging Christians place a premium on community, on living life together in all its messiness. However, community can take many shapes, and emerging or altworship communities often do not resemble traditional church community with a paid staff and centralized leadership. It's a dispersed community, a patchwork of enclaves dotting the landscape of contemporary culture. Members live together, love together, and dream together in the rough-and-tumble of everyday life.

Transformation

Emerging types are passionate about transformation, both personal and structural. They tend not to view themselves as finished products, as "saved" or even as "Christian." Instead, they speak of themselves as "*being* saved" and "*becoming* Christian." They tend to be political activists and socially "liberal" in the sense that they care deeply about the proverbial "widow, orphan, and alien"—those who are marginalized, oppressed, and disenfranchised—and about changing the personal and structural realities that perpetuate the disenfranchisement and marginalization. They believe that engaging in such tasks is not supplemental to following Jesus but is an essential part of what it *means* to follow Jesus. And they don't much care who you are or what you believe: if you're laboring for the poor, the marginalized, and the disenfranchised, then you're doing God's work, and that's what matters here and now.

Worship

Emerging Christians are innovative and imaginative in the aesthetics of worship, and they are technologically savvy. They're sacramental and incarnational, sometimes employing large-scale transformative theater, such as the ikon community does in Northern Ireland. I say sacramental and incarnational because of the heavy emphasis on the tactility of emerging worship and emerging living. God, Christians believe, became incarnate, wrapped himself in ordinary human skin and bone. Emerging Christians believe God is still revealing himself in the ordinary and earthy. And their worship embodies this incarnational and tactile character.

Revelation, one of the communities we visited in London, for example, offers a sophisticated blend of ancient ritual and liturgy and cutting-edge image technology and participation. Worship that engages us as whole and embodied beings, providing a feast for most if not all of our sensory modalities—sight, sound, taste, smell, and touch—is typical in these communities. (You'll get a small taste of this in the footage from the accompanying DVD.)

Social Engagement

Emerging Christians enthusiastically endorse Jesus's claim that "by their fruits you will know them." Thus, they seek to be active agents of God's reconciling, redemptive, and restorative agenda in and for the world. They are thus politically and socially engaged.

It should be pointed out that the emerging church movement resonates not so much with a particular demographic (e.g., well-to-do twenty- and thirtysomethings) so much as with what a friend of mine has described as a particular *psycho*-graphic (i.e., with people in their twenties, thirties, forties, fifties, sixties, and even seventies who share a certain cultural aesthetic and cultural sensibility). So it's a mistake, I think, to suggest that the movement is a youth movement or appeals only to a younger generation.

It is also decidedly not a movement peculiar to evangelical Protestants. It is popping up among people all across the denominational landscape: Protestant, evangelical nondenominational, Episcopal, and Roman Catholics alike. And while some talk about how long a run emerging Christianity will have, I suggest that its "demise" is actually written in its DNA. The emerging church is much like a flash mob that comes together in a certain place at a certain time and for a limited duration. However long emerging Christianity lasts, you can bet its DNA will turn up in future incarnations of church and theology.

Book Overview

This volume is divided into four parts, consisting of two chapters each. The first part, "Philosophy," opens with my "Who's Afraid of Philosophical Realism? Taking Emerging Christianity to Task." In it I explore emerging authors' and practitioners' allergy to philosophical realism and to creedal formulations of Christian belief. I suggest that this situation derives largely from either a confusion of *epistemic humility* with philosophical *antirealism* (terms clearly defined in the chapter) or the mistaken belief that the epistemic humility that emerging Christians prize depends on postmodern, philosophical antirealism. I argue that commitment to ecumenical creedal formulations and to concrete Christian beliefs is in no way incompatible with or inimical to epistemic humility or other distinctive features of postmodernity prized by emerging Christians, such as the deep conviction that our grasp of reality is always partial, incomplete, and provisional. Since what seems to lie at the heart of emerging sensibility is epistemic humility, and not relativistic, creative antirealism, I call for an embrace of what might be termed *chastened realism*. I also call for a respectful division of philosophical labor within emerging circles between so-called analytic and continental styles of philosophy by suggesting that deconstructive philosophy and analytic philosophy, or what I want to call *clarificatory philosophy*, are complementary, noncompeting modes of discourse.

The second chapter, "The Worldly Theology of Emerging Christianity," by Peter Rollins, argues for the claim that emerging thought is first and foremost a critique of Christianity as *hermeneutical*, that is, a privileged way of interpreting the world. Rollins challenges us to replace this view with an approach that seeks to symbolically enact the divine kenosis (*self-emptying*), in other words performatively emptying ourselves of our various religious and political interpretations of reality and thus taking on the identity of Christ, who in the incarnation became nothing. Rollins argues that it is in this desertlike space of negation that we are transformed and Christianity rightly seen not as a privileged way of *interpreting* or *knowing* the world but rather as a way of *changing* the world.

Chapter 3 opens the second part of the volume, "Theology," with "Consumer Liturgies and Their Corrosive Effects on Christian Identity," by Jason Clark, who argues that consumer society is rife with identity-forming liturgical practices and that Christians are not immune to its identity-forming effects. From the consumer calendar, which provides the rhythm, and the shopping malls, which provide the secular space for engaging in the practices of consumption, to the lengths to which we go to discipline our bodies, our characters are being shaped by the narrative of consumption. Emerging communities must be places, therefore, that offer alternative liturgies, ones that cultivate peculiarly Christian characters and fortify Christians to live in the world without being of the world.

In chapter 4, "Thy Kingdom Come (on Earth): An Emerging Eschatology," I explore the biblical notion of the kingdom of God—an unexpected, unanticipated, and often iconoclastic in-breaking event that brings about a new reality. Through an examination of the concept of "kingdom of God," I draw out the richly textured contours of a new Jerusalem and show how emerging Christianity can be understood first and foremost as an eschatological movement, a vibrant anticipatory enactment of a new reality, namely, God's kingdom come, and still coming.

The fifth chapter opens part 3, "Worship." Here Jason Clark kicks things off with his essay "The Renewal of Liturgy in the Emerging Church." Clark argues that it is not enough to provide worship aesthetics and experiences to help make sense of life; instead, all Christian worship—emerging or not—is about the right ordering of life and the formation and embodiment of our identity as Christ followers. Emerging collectives therefore must provide liturgies that invite us to participate in, repeat, and enact together as a community practices that remind us of who we are and who God is. The story these rituals and practices enact, moreover, is not of our own choosing (i.e., another consumer choice we make). Rather, Clark argues that Christian liturgies open those who practice them to the possibility of reconnecting with the Christian story—and with the people who have held and practiced it through the ages—so that we ourselves might also know and incarnate the story in our own peculiarly postmodern communities and spheres of influence.

In chapter 6, "Transformance Art: Reconfiguring the Social Self," Peter Rollins draws on the thought of Nietzsche and Heidegger to describe emerging collectives as groups engaging in innovative ways to help close the gap between belief and practice through *transfor-*

mance art. The essay explores the nature of the ironic stance, which is a way of intellectually distancing ourselves from social activities that we might willingly engage in but that actually undermine the very commitments we profess to hold most dear. Rollins shows how the practices of transformance art of emerging collectives are designed to combat the ironic stance.

In chapters 7 and 8, Scot McKnight addresses issues in both the Bible and doctrine. In "Scripture in the Emerging Movement," Mc-Knight sketches ways Christians read the Bible—as a law book, as a collection of blessings and promises, as a Rorschach inkblot, as a massive puzzle, and through the lens of one author, who is treated as a maestro. An emerging understanding of Scripture recognizes that language is being asked to carry an enormous load in speaking for God and of God. McKnight brings into this context the recent and brilliant work of the Jewish scholar Michael Fishbane, who draws us into the potency of language while recognizing that all language eventually drains itself dry before the "unsayable God." Scripture, McKnight argues, needs to be approached as a collection of wiki-stories of *the* Story. We know the plot, but the Story itself is known only through the particular wiki-stories (the individual authors of the Bible who tell the Story in their books).

"Atonement and Gospel" brings the volume to a close. Here Mc-Knight notes that there is a marked focus today among some to speak of both double imputation and propitiation as either the center of the atonement or the most important idea contained in the concept of atonement. The remarkable problem is that double imputation is never unambiguously taught in the New Testament, and propitiation is rarely taught. Moreover, when double imputation and propitiation are made the gospel message, preaching involves the framing of our problem as guilt and being under the wrath of God. And this, McKnight argues, leads to the presentation of Christ's death and the gospel as the event whereby God's wrath is appeased (propitiation) and our guilt removed. But that's not the gospel, McKnight suggests. In this chapter, McKnight attempts to recapture just what the gospel message of the Bible actually is.

All of these issues and topics are interesting in their own right. Insofar as they form several of the substantive issues in emerging conversations and reflection, they are crucial both for understanding what the emerging church is and where it is going. One of the aims of this volume is to give the reader a front-row seat as four scholars in philosophy, theology, and biblical studies frame and discuss these important topics.

Philosophy | Part 1

1

Who's Afraid of Philosophical Realism?

Taking Emerging Christianity to Task

KEVIN CORCORAN

Emerging and emerging-friendly books, conversations, blogs, and seminars exhibit a tendency to look askance at something that goes by the name *realism*. There is also an allergy to creeds and creedal formulations of Christian beliefs due to a sense that the language and concepts produced by finite human beings simply cannot capture, contain, or express anything abiding and true when it comes to the infinite and iconoclastic God of Christian theism. Alongside a rejection of realism and a soft spot for so-called apophatic, or negative, theology, there is a deep and sincere epistemological humility among emerging folk.

I suggest in this essay that participants in emerging conversations do not distinguish between these three issues—realism, an allergy to creeds and beliefs, and epistemic humility. Or if they do distinguish between them, they either mistake epistemic humility *for* antirealism or falsely believe that embracing epistemic humility *requires* that they embrace antirealism and reject or refuse to embrace concrete Christian beliefs. This, I will try to show, is false. While I believe that epistemic humility most certainly ought to be embraced with the enthusiasm and zeal that emerging Christians bring to all their endeavors, Christians who take the postmodern cultural context seriously *should not* and indeed *need not* embrace antirealism. And as to the issue of negative theology and the rejection of creedal formulations, I suggest that confessing particular beliefs about God—and the positive theology that results—does not entail any pretense on the part of the believer that such beliefs domesticate or otherwise pin God down; nor does it require renouncing the epistemic humility that emerging Christians rightly prize. Therefore, the rallying cry of emerging Christians who call for creating a religion without religion or a church "beyond belief" is, I suggest, a call we need not and indeed ought not heed.

Confession/Autobiography

I write this essay from the perspective of one very favorably disposed to forms of Christian faith and practice that participants in emerging cohorts, collectives, and conversations engage in. I participate in many of them; I read the blogs, occasionally blog myself at www.holyskinandbone.blogspot.com, and find myself quite comfortable among that growing number of Christians seeking ever more authentic and culturally engaged ways of expressing and practicing their faith, following Jesus, and rethinking or reimagining church for the world in the twenty-first century. I also desire to do so in ways that honor the inheritance and authority of some two thousand years of Christian history; this tradition and reflection, as well as my desire to honor it, may put me on a path that not everyone within emerging Christianity follows—or is even interested in following. Fair enough. I'm simply registering up front my own biases.

I offer this essay, therefore, as a friendly critique of emerging Christianity. The title, "Who's Afraid of Philosophical Realism: Taking Emerging Christianity to Task," is a takeoff, of course, of my colleague Jamie Smith's very fine book *Who's Afraid of Postmodernism? Taking*

Derrida, Lyotard, and Foucault to Church, itself a takeoff of Derrida's book *Who's Afraid of Philosophy?* I chose the title because it seems to me that, just as many traditional and evangelical Christians are unnecessarily afraid of postmodernism, many postmodern emerging Christians are likewise unnecessarily afraid of philosophical realism.

Before digging into the issues, permit me to engage in a little spiritual autobiography and to share with you how I came to be involved in the so-called emerging church. In 2004, I experienced something of a midlife crisis. My midlife crisis, however, did not manifest itself in my quitting my job as a newly tenured philosophy professor and trying to become a rock star or an accomplished chef. I didn't trade in my Honda Civic for a new convertible or take up with a woman twenty years my junior. I did, I suppose, begin to trade in old wineskins for new. But the old wineskins were habits of thinking and ways of being in the world, and the new skins I was trading for were also habits of thinking and ways of being in the world—different habits and ways of being in the world than those that I was discovering could no longer hold the wine they were designed to carry.

For me a specific event precipitated the crisis, an event that upended things, undid me, and ruptured my world. I found myself, as a result, disoriented, baffled, confused, perplexed, and as a blessed result, ripe for radical transformation. I would come to discover that many of the beliefs and ideals that I had clung to for years as a Christian, beliefs and ideals that gave my life a kind of coherence and stability, had flown under the radar of my conscious awareness and reflection and were, at the end of the day and despite being good and admirable ideals, actually idols, fictions of my own making, unreliable gods that I substituted for the iconoclastic God of Abraham, Isaac, Jacob, and Jesus.

It was in that space of having been broken open, that space of disorientation and confusion, where the truth about myself was laid painfully bare to me—much like the truth about Sheppard is made painfully bare to him at the end of Flannery O'Connor's short story "The Lame Shall Enter First"—that I discovered myself to be in the midst of spiritual rebirth. Indeed, the years from 2004 to 2007, although without doubt three of the most difficult of my life, were probably the most spiritually invigorating. And while it is true that we live our lives forward only to understand them backward, I was very much aware of being reconfigured, reoriented, and I hoped, reintegrated. It was during those years that I found myself listening to others or, in the parlance of the postmodern, listening to *the other* in a way that I hadn't before. I had always *heard* the stories of those who inhabited different skin and ways of being in the world, but perhaps for the first time, I found myself really *listening* and being changed by them. I had, I suppose, become more supple, gracious, and forgiving as a result of my own crisis. And then I began to read books by some of these others, whose books I wouldn't have read before those years; one of them was by a guy named Brian McLaren. Strangely, I thought, I found myself resonating with much of what I was reading and hearing. I was especially moved by *The Story We Find Ourselves In*.

In any case, there was a time in my life when labels really mattered to me. What am I? Am I evangelical or Reformed, conservative or liberal? But I was coming to discover that labels didn't seem to matter much anymore—religious, political, philosophical, whatever. And I was discovering others who were coming to the same sorts of conclusions, and on a whole range of issues.

Moreover, in those years I was becoming much more interested in what might be called "the ordinary business of life," of anticipating in the concrete world, in the concrete reality of one's own lived experience, that new reality that Christ spoke of and indeed embodied. One thing led to another, and I began to meet lots of people who seemed to be drinking from the same postmodern wells as I was, cisterns of story, collaboration, humility, and mystery. These people seemed to possess an honesty and authenticity that I really had not experienced before. Feeling myself bent and broken, confused and reeling, I found their honesty and authenticity enormously refreshing. I started a group in Grand Rapids called In Vino Theologica (in wine there is theology). It was a motley group of people—Catholic, Protestant, Eastern Orthodox, and religious skeptics alike—all coming together to think about and wrestle with God. We were young and old (or at least not as young), male and female, married, unmarried, and divorced. We still meet, in fact. We've lost some members to job relocations and college graduation, and we've gained new ones. What we all have in common is a realization that we are all *pilgrims on the way*, that there is much to learn and much to be gained from wrestling with God in the company of others and the bonds of friendship.

The more I talked with people, people I was meeting all across the country and outside it, face-to-face and via the world wide web, the more convinced I was becoming that something big was under way. That something for me was a new chapter in my own pilgrimage. Phyllis Tickle has given that something a name: *The Great Emergence.* Maybe it's the Marxist in me (that of the Groucho sort!)—the fact that I don't want to be a member of any club that would have me as a member—that explains my impatience with the question whether I am an "emerging Christian." Like the first Christians, who did not *call* themselves Christians but were *called* Christian, I will leave it to others to label me. The only label I will lay claim to, and with a generous amount of fear and trembling, is the label of Christ follower. I claim that label with fear and trembling because I'm not very good at it. I'm still working on it, still learning the vocabulary and grammar, still cultivating the habits. In any case, this is the circuitous road that led me to my acquaintance with the emerging church.

What follows is a critique of one feature of what is called emerging Christianity, a stream of Christian faith and practice that I find a most hospitable environment.

The Issues

Let's cut right to the chase. What is philosophical realism? What does it imply? What doesn't it imply? And how about postmodernism? Emerging, if it is anything at all, is most definitely *postmodern.* But what on earth is postmodernism? Frankly, the term *postmodern* has to rank among the most overused and least understood locutions in popular philosophy and theology. It could be argued, in fact, that *postmodernism* is even less meaningful and helpful than the term *evangelical*, if that's possible. And yet the term or concept plays a significant role in emerging conversations and self-ascription without so much as a definition or elucidation, as if its meaning were self-evident. It is crucial, therefore, that we get as clear as possible on these important terms if we are going to employ them meaningfully.

Philosophical Realism

Let's begin with philosophical realism. What is it? To begin, let's consider: I am inclined to think that there is, say, God and our various understandings of God (e.g., I believe that God is loving and merciful and gracious etc.). I am also inclined to think that there are the various objects of my perceptual experience, like stars and mountains and mollusks, and our concepts of those objects. One might say, therefore, that I am a *realist* regarding God, stars, mountains, and mollusks, since I believe that such objects exist quite *apart from* and *independent of* the conceptual contributions of minded beings like us. In other words, I may have *mistaken* beliefs about God or stars or mollusks and what have you. But I believe that the things about which I may have mistaken beliefs actually exist. Such things (if such there be) would be *discovered*, or if not, at least *not* manufactured by human language and practice.

It is important to note, of course, that such things as God, stars, mountains, and mollusks *differ* from such things as computers, cars, and cattle prods. I'm a realist about the latter as well. But the difference is that the existence of the latter objects (unlike the existence of the former) has *everything* to do with minded beings like us. Indeed, if there were no minded beings like us, such things never would have existed. Not so with God and stars and mountains and mollusks. The *existence* (or nonexistence) of these things has nothing to do with human *social* practices. So says the realist, at any rate.

In contrast to philosophical realism, there is what we might call *creative antirealism*, or *irrealism*, as it is sometimes called. According to creative antirealism, our concepts and language actually *create* such things as God (if such there be) and the objects that populate the world, like stars, mountains, and mollusks, no less than computers, cars, and cattle prods. In other words, contrary to what most of us believe, we don't *discover* stars, mountains, or mollusks, or their properties, in the world and then use language and concepts to refer to them and describe them; we *create* them with our words, concepts, and social practices. Philosophers often put it like this: there is no objectively existing world *out there*, existing independently of the *subjective* human knower or cognizer; the whole subject-object dichotomy is a fiction, a useful fiction perhaps but a fiction nonetheless.

There is a slightly tamer version of the social-constructive variety of antirealism. According to it, while there may be a world independent of our concepts and language, we are simply constitutionally incapable of ever coming to know it as it is, independent of us. As this relates to God, the idea is something like this: God is so big, so wholly *other*, and we are so small (or finite), that to *name* God as loving or merciful or gracious (or whatever) is really to create an idol; it always results in an unsuccessful attempt to domesticate or tame the untameable, to *name* the unnameable God. It makes God a mere *object* of theological fetish.

Social-constructive antirealism is a tamer version of creative antirealism because it acknowledges that some things may indeed exist independent of our interests and practices; it's just that our own sociocultural limitations, among other things, prevent us from saying anything about things *as they are apart from us*. Thus, those attracted to this tamer version of antirealism are also attracted to what is called *apophatic*, or negative, theology, the view that God, as God is in himself, remains always unknown and unknowable. Meister Eckhart, the late thirteenth-century Christian mystic, captures what is at the heart of the apophatic sensibility: "It is the hidden darkness of the eternal divinity, and it is unknown, and it was never known, and it never will be known. God remains there within himself, unknown."[1] Indeed, the proper but difficult task of (postmodern) theology is to rid our mind of its idols (i.e., our names for and descriptions of God). For this will make way for the *event* of God. For again, God is not in this view a mere *object* to be dissected and parsed like a specimen under the scientist's microscope. Rather, God is a life-transformative and life-altering *subjective event*.

Postmodernism: The Big Picture

So much for apophaticism, realism, and creative antirealism. Before I offer an assessment of those, let us consider postmodernism. What is it? A common understanding of postmodernism has it that a cataclysmic, epochal shift occurred in the fairly recent past, when we moved from "modernism," or a modernist way of viewing the world, to "postmodernism," or a postmodern way of viewing the world. This sort of take on postmodernism is advanced by Neo in Brian McLaren's *A New Kind of Christian*[2] and by Tony Jones in *The New Christians*[3] and also by Stanley Grenz in *A Primer on Postmodernism*.[4] Here's how Robert Webber describes it in *The Divine Embrace*: "In the postmodern world, the way of knowing has changed. We now live in a world in which people have lost interest in argument and have taken to story, imagination, mystery, ambiguity, and vision."[5]

According to this view, modernism came to full flower in the Enlightenment era, when reason was exalted above all, and confidence in the ability to transcend one's own sociocultural-historical context *through the use of reason alone* was meeting with startling confirmation. Remarkable successes in scientific discovery and mastery of nature provided fuel to the modernist fire. It was looking more and more like the natural world was giving up its most intimate secrets to reason and that through science and technology, reason's most natural employer, we human beings were on the precipice of solving humanity's most pressing problems—physical, social, and otherwise.

Then, at some point in the fairly recent past, everything supposedly changed. Central to this putative epochal shift in how we view the world is the academic and abstruse work of philosophers on the continent of Europe, especially the French philosophers Jacques Derrida and Jean-François Lyotard. The changes—their calling into question the mechanistic view of nature peculiar to modernism, the pretense of reason, a knower's ability to transcend its radical particularity and to view the world from a God's-eye perspective—are said to rival the changes of the Copernican revolution in science.

I am not sure what to make of these claims. The putatively "epic" nature of the shift strikes me as overexaggerated. I have no doubt about there being differences, and significant differences at that, between this generation and previous generations. But I am inclined to think that those differences are largely cultural and actually have little to do with the philosophical ruminations of the patron saints of so-called deconstructive philosophy, Derrida and Lyotard, with whom postmodernism is so often associated.

Postmodernism: Zeroing In

That's the big picture. It contains a claim about the putative significance of postmodernism. And as I say, I'm not sure what to make of it. But let's zero in on a definition of postmodernism. I begin by distinguishing between *cultural* postmodernism and *philosophical* postmodernism. If the cultural icons of modernity were the factory, industry, manufacturing, and the production of goods, then the cultural markers of postmodernism are information, new technologies (e.g., cell phones and the internet, with their ubiquitous social networking capabilities), connectivity, interdependence, decentralization, and globalization. These features of postmodernism are, I think, very significant. Epic? Maybe. I don't know. Time, I guess, will tell.

Philosophical postmodernism, on the other hand, involves calling into question "metanarratives," or grand stories of the world and our place in it, like Marxism, atheistic naturalism, consumerism, and Christianity itself. In other words, philosophical postmodernism questions our ability to float free of the grand narratives we find ourselves in and to view things from a "God's-eye view." In this sense, postmodernism is a flat-out rejection of what is at the heart of the Enlightenment ideal, that is, the dispassionate, unbiased, and transcendent ego grasping reality by use of unvarnished reason.

Those sensitive to this aspect of postmodernism recognize that our grasp of reality is always *partial, incomplete*, and *fragmentary*. We are, after all, situated beings, limited in many ways—by history, by geography, by gender, by time. And reason is likewise tethered and bound. A recognition of these facts can engender humility, tolerance, and an opening for dialogue with others. Those who really appreciate our human finitude and situatedness are more inclined to say, "Here's how I see things and here's why. But I recognize that I am a finite and frail human being, so I could certainly be the one with blind spots. How do you see things?" as opposed to saying "I'm right. You're wrong and going to hell. End of story."

If this is how we are to understand philosophical postmodernism, then count me in, as this flavor of postmodernism resonates deeply with me, and if I read Tony Jones and other "new" Christians right, it resonates deeply with them too.

And yet there is another element or aspect some people (including some in the emerging movement) often add to this plausible rendering of postmodernism. And that is what I have called in a previous section *creative antirealism*, or social constructivism. Those who add this element to postmodernism do so, it seems to me, because they believe either that the epistemic humility characteristic of the plausible strain of postmodernism requires it or that the plausible form of postmodernism leads to it. It does not. And it's easy to see why.

Epistemic Humility and Creative Antirealism

The claim that our grasp of reality is always partial, incomplete, and fragmentary, and the humility, tolerance, and dialogue that flow from such a realization do not require a corresponding commitment to creative antirealism. A firm grasp of our *creatureliness*—from which follows the fact that we humans are finite, frail, and fallible—I contend is sufficient in itself to engender a robust sort of epistemic humility. Frail, fallible, finite creatures that we are, our grasp of reality—including God—will never rise above that frailty, finitude, and fallibility. There is therefore no need to embrace the creative antirealism so often associated with postmodernism when the resources for epistemic humility are present in the Christian tradition itself. Indeed, it is the flip side of our status as *creatures*—namely, the Christian conviction of God as *Creator*—that is most hospitable to philosophical realism. For while it is true that God has endowed us with morally significant freedom, the use of which has resulted in the creation of culture and the artifactual world of automobiles and atom bombs, it is also the same God who created the natural world of mountains and streams, salamanders and solar systems. And it is God who has created us as part of the natural world and outfitted us with the means of both grasping and stewarding that world. So, realism, yes! Epistemic humility? Yes too. It is the Christian story itself that grounds a realist view of the world and our finitude and frailty that ought to chasten our claims to knowledge.

The antirealist and apophatic elements, often layered over the plausible form of postmodernism, lead many emerging Christians to call for a Christianity *beyond* belief. The idea is that committing oneself to concrete Christian beliefs places oneself in the primordial waters of modernism and the pretentious grip of the Enlightenment ideal. As the writer of *The Cloud of Unknowing* so succinctly put it: "God may well be loved but not thought" (chap. 54). The postmodern turn for Christians is, therefore, a turn away from Christianity as *believing* or *knowing* certain things and a turn toward Christianity as opening oneself up to a transformative *event*. To put it another way, it is a turn away from faith as a kind of *scientia* (knowledge) and a turn toward faith as a kind of *sapientia* (wisdom), wisdom construed more in terms of the subjective and affective than the objective and cognitive. As I read them, both Spencer Burke[6] and Peter Rollins[7] advocate such a view.

An example might be helpful. What is the relationship between philosophical realism and religious experience? One might think that the relation is a loose one at best. The problem is that the relation might indeed be a loose one on one level but not so loose on another. For example, one might think that what is important is not that the resurrection occurred as a historical event but that Jesus rises as a subjective, transformative event or experience in the lives of his followers.

At the level of reflective theorizing, *if* Jesus did not rise, then those who claim to have been transformed by an encounter *with* the risen Christ are mistaken. People who say they've had such an experience may in fact have experienced a transformative event, but if Christ is not risen, then their transformation does not owe to an event involving the resurrected Christ. If this is so, it leaves open the very real possibility of people participating in an event involving the risen Christ without those people realizing that it is an encounter *with* the risen Christ. The point is this: *if* the event has anything to do *with* a risen Christ, then Christ must be risen.

Let me put it this way: at the conceptual level, the level of reflective theorizing, the literal resurrection of Jesus has a kind of priority over experience insofar as an experience of the resurrected Christ *requires* (logically or conceptually) a resurrected Christ to be experienced.

On the other hand, and at the level of the phenomenology of religious experience, Christianity is a *subjective*, transformative *event* that upends, ruptures, and transforms human life. At this level, much like the blind man in John 9, we may find ourselves simply able to say, "One thing I do know, that though I was blind, now I see" (John 9:25). At this level, debate about whether Jesus *really* rose from the dead might seem like the wrong question. At the level of lived experience, asked whether Jesus really and literally rose from the dead, we can imagine a follower of Christ saying, "Well, I *believe* he rose from the dead. I mean, this experience I've had seemed to involve him."

Let me bring all this back down to earth with a bit of autobiography. When I think of a biblical story that parallels my own life experience, I think of the story of Peter out in the boat and Jesus calling him to himself, calling him to get out of the boat and to come toward him. Peter must have been terrified. I feel like Peter a lot of the time, in the sense that I feel as if I've received a call (from Jesus), but between him and me is a raging storm, or to switch metaphors, between him and me is a thick woods. I cannot see clearly most of the time. So I am doing my best (and sometimes less than my best) to make my way toward that voice, toward the one issuing the call.

As I understand it, mine is not a faith that is a groping toward an *I-know-not-what*. Mine is a faith that is most definitely a groping, but a groping toward a God of all-inclusive love, compassion, and mercy, who was, I believe, in Christ reconciling the world to himself and bringing about a new reality, a new society. A robust recognition that I am a finite creature, frail and given to self-deception, and that my knowledge of God and the world is thus always partial, fragmentary, and incomplete, does not lead me to *religious skepticism*. It leads me to *epistemic humility*. And epistemic humility is perfectly compatible with concrete Christian beliefs and commitments. But this raises a few important questions: What is the relation between belief and practice? Which is or ought to have priority? Is Christianity fundamentally about ortho*doxy* or ortho*praxy*?

Belief or Practice?

The Christian faith, I would argue, is fundamentally about spiritual formation; it is concerned with a radical reorientation and redirection of our desires, our loves, our hates, our very lives. It is no surprise therefore that, for fifteen hundred years of Christian history, practices, rituals, sacraments, feasts, and fasts served as the primary means for the redirection and reorientation of our lives, for our spiritual formation as icons of God and followers of Jesus, whose end is communion with God and others. Only since the Reformation has the pendulum swung away from the embodied practices of concrete communities as central to spiritual formation and toward the atomistic, disembodied, and cerebral-centered. I suggest that it's time for the pendulum to swing in the opposite direction once again.

When it comes to faith I am, after all these years, still a beginner. I am always ever a beginner. I am coming to see, I guess, that I am still *learning* to believe, still *learning how* to believe. For a long time, I was preoccupied with *what* to believe. As I get older I am coming to see that *how* I believe is of equal importance. I am coming to see that belief is something that takes practice and something one learns to do over time. Here it is worth quoting at some length the thought of Stanley Hauerwas. In his essay "Discipleship as Craft: Church as a Disciplined Community," he compares becoming a Christian to the art of bricklaying. He says,

> To learn to lay brick, it is not sufficient for you to be told how to do it; you must learn to mix the mortar, build scaffolds, joint, and so on. Moreover, it is not enough to be told how to hold a trowel, how to spread mortar, or how to frog the mortar. In order to lay brick you must hour after hour, day after day, lay brick.
>
> Of course, learning to lay brick involves learning not only myriad skills, but also a language that forms, and is formed by those skills. Thus, for example, you have to become familiar with what a trowel is and how it is to be used, as well as mortar, which bricklayers usually call "mud." Thus "frogging mud" means creating a trench in the mortar so that when the brick is placed in the mortar, a vacuum is created that almost makes the brick lay itself. Such language is not just incidental to becoming a bricklayer but is intrinsic to the practice. You cannot learn to lay brick without learning to talk "right."
>
> The language embodies the history of the craft of bricklaying. So when you learn to be a bricklayer you are not learning a craft de novo but rather being initiated into a history. For example, bricks have different names—klinkers, etc.—to denote different qualities that make a difference about how one lays them. These differences are often discovered

by apprentices being confronted with new challenges, making mistakes, and then being taught how to do the work by the more experienced.[8]

Now the comparison:

> Christianity is not beliefs about God plus behavior. We are Christians not because of what we believe, but because we have been called to be disciples of Jesus. To become a disciple is not a matter of a new or changed self-understanding, but rather to become part of a different community with a different set of practices.
>
> For example, I am sometimes confronted by people who are not Christians but who say they want to know about Christianity. This is a particular occupational hazard for theologians around a university, because it is assumed that we are smart or at least have a Ph.D., so we must really know something about Christianity. After many years of vain attempts to "explain" God as trinity, I now say, "Well, to begin with we Christians have been taught to pray, 'Our father, who art in heaven . . .'" I then suggest that a good place to begin to understand what we Christians are about is to join me in that prayer.
>
> For to learn to pray is no easy matter but requires much training, not unlike learning to lay brick. It does no one any good to believe in God, at least the God we find in Jesus of Nazareth, if they have not learned to pray. To learn to pray means we must acquire humility not as something we try to do, but as commensurate with the practice of prayer. In short, we do not believe in God, become humble and then learn to pray, but in learning to pray we humbly discover we cannot do other than believe in God.[9]

Now this is not to say that beliefs are unimportant; indeed, it is perfectly compatible with saying that beliefs are of fundamental importance. It is not to suggest that we can't say anything meaningful about God either. It is to point out that becoming a Christian is not about the beliefs. Christianity is about the reconfiguration of the human heart, the redirection of human desire. Christianity crucially involves beliefs, but it's not about the beliefs. Because the Christian faith is about lives well lived in conformity with our created nature, the Christian faith inducts Christians into concrete practices, rituals, and sacraments that had for over fifteen hundred years of Christian history the life-transforming effect of producing Christian disciples.

And the importance of ritualized practices and sacraments is not lost on emerging Christians.

An Alliance of Deconstructive and Analytic Modes of Discourse

I think it's important that we get as clear as we can about what we're talking about when we talk about postmodernism. If the postmodernism of emerging Christians is the more plausible version of philosophical postmodernism I described above, then I am on board. If it is the postmodernism of creative antirealism, I am not. And what of apophaticism? I think our language can apply quite literally to God and that because of God's self disclosure, or God's having spoken to us, we can say things that are true about God. For example, I think we can confess the content of the Apostles' Creed and justifiably believe that we are speaking the truth about God. Which is not to say that human language can ever exhaustively describe God or that our beliefs about God can ever be more than provisional. Even the content of the Apostles' Creed has this feature. As the archbishop of Canterbury has said with respect to the Apostles' Creed, "It's the least silly things we can say about God." I believe that God really is *loving* and *compassionate* and *just*. I am sure I cannot plumb the depths of God's love and compassion and justice with words or concepts. But I also don't think that when we get to heaven (or heaven in all its fullness gets to us) we will discover that God is so wholly other, and our language so completely impotent, that it turns out God is really self-absorbed, hateful, wicked, unjust, and apathetic.

Let us return for a moment to the earlier quote of Robert Webber's: "In the postmodern world, the way of knowing has changed. We now live in a world in which people have lost interest in argument and have taken to story, imagination, mystery, ambiguity, and vision." I suggest, contrary to Webber, that not very much has changed over time with respect to how we human beings come to belief. The world—premodern, modern, and postmodern—was never such that *most* people came to believe very many things by way of argument. Read Plato's *Republic* (fourth century before Christ), for example, or any of his dialogues. They are not treasure troves of careful argumentation. They are instead rife with stories. Read the Bible itself. More stories. And the popularity of stories—personal stories—can hardly be exaggerated. Have a look at the recent sale statistics of personal memoirs, for example.

That story—not argument—is what captures the human heart and imagination, what moves us, and what serves as a significant mode of belief is not unique to postmodernity. And whereas mystery and ambiguity can seem more like ways of *un*knowing, *story* surely seems to be one very important sort of invitation to belief. In fact, the most important thing I've ever come to believe I came to believe through story, not argument. What is this most important thing? It is this: "Jesus loves me this I know, for the Bible tells me so. Yes, Jesus loves me. Yes, Jesus loves me. Yes, Jesus loves me; the Bible tells me so." The Bible tells me so not in syllogism and argument, but, again, in story, complex stories involving all the ambiguity, pathos, mixed motives, and twisted intentions that characterize human life in human skin.

Having said that, I agree that mystery and ambiguity seem today to be valorized and readily embraced more so than in days gone by. But they are not actually ways of knowing. Rather, they function more at the level of a psychological milieu, a milieu that is more hospitable to story, liturgy, and sacrament than to syllogism and argument. Story, liturgy, and sacrament engage us much more holistically than does argument. They engage the *affective*, the *passional*, and the *sensual* dimensions of human existence, whereas argument seems to engage us almost exclusively along the cognitive-cerebral dimension. So those whose experience of life and God have the feel and flavor of mystery and ambiguity will resonate more readily with story, liturgy, sacrament, and the imaginative.

Here's what Webber goes on to say following the ellipses in the paragraph above: "However, this does not mean or at least should not mean the complete loss of reason. Reason has a place in story. It is Christian rationalism that has failed, not intelligent discourse."[10] It is easy to skate uncomprehending over that sentence. But we ought not. Instead, we should pause and linger over it for a bit. For in this neighborhood we find our entrée into a harmonious alliance of the deconstructive and analytic modes of discourse.

Reason and Argument

In the sound-bite culture postmodernity has helped to create, intelligent discourse is failing. Mystery, ambiguity, and story are all good and fine—indispensable even—but there are public spaces, occasions, and contexts where argumentation is both necessary and vital. And one such space is the public square of debate concerning how to negotiate an increasingly pluralistic and global society. However, to a culture with the attention span of a squirrel, a consumer culture characterized by fragmentation, montage, and sound bite, the features of nuance, care, and settling in with a lengthy text—features characteristic of argumentation in the best sense of that term—are considered difficult, annoying, and, well, downright "modern."

To the extent that postmodernism involves deconstruction, and deconstruction involves memory and omission, our current cultural context, characterized by various sorts of pluralism, presents us with a deconstructive moment, a significant moment both for liberal democracies and religious faiths. Let me explain.

It is almost a commonplace to believe that deep commitment to a religious faith poses a threat to the liberal ideals at the heart of Western democracies. The idea that one's loyalties and allegiances can be, or should be allowed to be, split or shared is unthinkable. Yet for a person of religious faith living in a pluralistic society governed by the rule of law, one's loyalties are in fact split or shared. "I am Christian and I am an American." "I am Muslim and I am a British citizen." "I am Jewish and I am American." The identity-forming features of confessional religions like Christianity, Judaism, and Islam are threatening because it is believed that confessional religion threatens social cohesion. Religion is fine, the secularizers would have us believe, so long as it is kept in its cage, domesticated at home, taken out for leisurely strolls within synagogue, mosque, or church one day a week (or year), but we mustn't let it out of its cage to run amok in the public square. It must be kept on a leash, behind the fences, or in the house.

Anyone with the audacity to suggest in the face of the monopolizing claims of the state—and so to remind those of us with religious identities—that, with respect to who we are, we are *joint* species, dual citizens as it were, is bound to come under attack, as the archbishop of Canterbury discovered in February 2008, when he suggested that Britain make some accommodations to its Muslim citizens. He was, in fact, recommending that the state simultaneously recognize one's identity as a Christian, a Jew, or in this case a Muslim without in effect introducing into society barbaric tribalisms of various sorts.

The archbishop's remarks were complex and nuanced, but a close, attentive reading clearly reveals that he was not advocating the adoption of sharia law or suggesting a parallel legal system. The problem was (and is) that reading, dwelling with nuance and complexity—that is, the stuff of argument and analysis—doesn't play well in the sound-bite media culture. Making fine distinctions, crafting careful arguments, must have their place, however, especially in a pluralistic and increasingly global marketplace of ideas and identities.

My point here is that while I am glad that the Bible is not chock-full of arguments with propositions, premises, and conclusions, I am also enormously grateful for the clarity of argument. For nuance and argument are the economic currency of public discourse—not story, liturgy, and mystery. And to the extent that emerging faith is deeply *this* worldy, is deeply engaged in the larger culture, not content to be ghettoized, to that same extent emerging Christians should valorize what is the stock-in-trade of traditionally analytic modes of philosophical discourse. Webber was absolutely right: while ambiguity, mystery, and story are of profound importance in engaging the heart and the affections, this should not mean the *complete* loss of reason. Reason must have a place in story. Perhaps the rationalism that typified Christian apologetics of the 1980s has failed, but we cannot allow intelligent discourse to fail.

And this is why I believe that both continental and analytic modes of discourse are necessary. Analytic philosophy prizes precision, clarity, and careful argumentation. Words matter, and in increasingly pluralistic societies and an increasingly shrinking world, precision of thinking and speaking matter even more. Even within emerging Christianity itself, words matter. *Postmodern, realism, epistemic humility*: what we mean by these terms is very important. For example, some people believe that all disagreements are semantic disagreements. "Oh, you're just arguing semantics," they say. Sometimes that is true. Sometimes differences can be resolved just by clarifying what we mean when we employ words, the *same* words. Sometimes, however, it's not that two people are saying the same thing but using different words to say it. Sometimes two people are saying *different* things not simply saying the same thing differently. In such cases the tools of analytic philosophy can be most helpful in bringing clarity and precision to discussions.

Deconstructive philosophy, on the other hand, is, I believe, of more existential significance. It is inherently more religious in the sense that it operates at the level of lived experience, at the level of sociopolitical engagement, and at the level of the human heart.

Conclusion

Who's afraid of philosophical realism? Lots of people. But there is no more need to be afraid of philosophical realism than there is to be afraid of Anglo-analytic philosophy. Granted there have been, and continue to be, Anglo-analytic philosophers and philosophical realists who are less than humble, who are, sadly, arrogant, narrow-minded idolaters. But arrogance and idolatry are equal opportunity employers. What I have attempted to establish in this chapter is that philosophical realism is quite hospitable to features essential to the emerging sensibility: epistemic humility; a rejection of the pretense of reason; and a spirit of openness, dialogue, and collaboration.

2

The Worldly Theology
of Emerging Christianity

PETER ROLLINS

Neither/Nor

The apostle Paul famously remarks that in Christ Jesus "there is neither Jew nor Greek, slave nor free, male nor female" (Gal. 3:28). Instead of writing about *both* Jews and Greeks, slaves and free, men and women, he writes of a new identity in Christ, one that cuts across political, cultural, and biological divisions, one that involves the laying down of such identities. This is not an expression of "both/and," in which we retain our identity when located in the new community of believers, but rather a "neither/nor," where we put aside those identities. In the new community founded by Christ, we find a sword has cut through such distinctions, opening up a different space.

Today this Pauline description of the community of believers can seem scandalous. In many churches we find flags proudly hanging in acknowledgment of our nationality, and we seek to express our particularistic political and religious ideas as a vital and irreducible part of who we are. We are proud of our heritage, our flag, our country, and we wish to take these with us into our places of worship. In short, we live in a time in which identity politics holds court.

But what if the church that Paul envisages in Galatians is one that calls into question the socio-symbolic identity of his readers? What if what Paul offers is a space that challenges distinctions such as Jew and Greek, male and female, slave and free? And what if Paul doesn't intend to stop with these three categories, as if they were the only ones abolished by Christ? What if he is implying that, in Christ, there is neither black nor white, neither rich nor poor, neither powerful nor powerless? What if we could go even further and say that the space Paul writes of is one in which there would be neither Republican nor Democrat, liberal nor conservative, orthodox nor heretic? Indeed, in the spirit of the text, what if we could offer an interpretive translation of Paul's words that would read,

> You are all children of God through faith in Christ Jesus, for all of you who were baptized into Christ have clothed yourselves with Christ. There is neither high church nor low church, Fox nor CNN, citizen nor alien, capitalist nor communist, gay nor straight, beautiful nor ugly, East nor West, theist nor atheist, Israeli nor Palestinian, hawk nor dove, American nor Iraqi, married nor divorced, uptown nor downtown, terrorist nor freedom fighter, priest nor prophet, fame nor obscurity, Christian nor non-Christian, for all are made one in Christ Jesus.

Of course, one of the problems with imagining a church that could express such radical unity amid diversity is the very nature of human beings as fundamentally in the world, that is, as constituted by the opaque socio-symbolic backgrounds we find ourselves in. I cannot really think outside my gender, my job, my sexual preferences, my political opinions, my nationality, and so on. These constitute *who* I am as a self-knowing subject. In this way some would counter that it would not merely be undesirable to live this idea of the neither/nor but also impossible. However, what if the event of Christ is so radical that it cuts through our presently existing socio-symbolic world, undermining what would seem to be the unchanging substance of our existence and opening up a new mode of being that does not conform to the structures of this world?

Some worry that such an idea does violence to our particularity. But far from attempting to pull back from the violence of this verse, perhaps we need to affirm it all the more strongly, especially in light of today's liberal Western environment, in which political action is focused on challenging injustice within the currently existing political system (fighting sexism in the workplace, racism in working-class estates, etc.) rather than challenging the very coordinates of the political system itself (which generates these problems in the first place). While much of the church is content to affirm the status quo, working for change within the system (e.g., giving money to the poor), Paul claims that, in Christ, we are also able to question the status quo (e.g., asking why the poor exist in the first place).

Although these verses suggest that identifying with Christ involves acknowledging that our socio-symbolic universe is contingent, this does not mean that it is no longer operative. Rather, to identity with Christ means to acknowledge that it is not the ultimate horizon. Here Paul suggests that the Christian community, while existing within the world, is called to place that world into question, to expose the truth that the ideologies grounding our world are not themselves grounded in some ultimate foundation. In other words, the church is called to expose the hegemonic ideology of the day as *contingent* and thus to provide the possibility of creating substantive societal change. For if identification with Christ involves shaking ourselves free from the structures of power defining the world, then we become free to think for ourselves and remake the world in new and liberating ways. When our minds are no longer conformed to the ideologies of this world, then we can begin to imagine and implement radical alternatives that help to bring substantive, though no less contingent, change to society.

In theological terms the enacting of this suspended space in which we call our socio-symbolic world into question can be described as a moment of participating in *kenosis*. This term can refer not only to the Christian idea of incarnation, in which the infinite dwells within the finite, but also to the "becoming nothing" of Jesus in his life as a servant, as one who stood outside the power structures of his age.

Suspended Space

One of the fundamental gifts that this nascent movement known
as emerging Christianity has to offer the wider church is a way of
concretely enacting this kenotic moment within the liturgical hour,
forming a space where people are invited to suspend their interpretations of the world.

In this space we are not invited to "fulfill our dreams" (i.e., the
dreams we have to improve society) but rather to dream new dreams.
The problem with attempting to fulfill our dreams relates to the limitation those attempts place on the scope of change itself. For our dreams
reflect our current values. These values are themselves reflections of
the cultural context we inhabit. The real challenge for us is to find
a space in which we are able to dream new dreams, reimagining the
kingdom of God in a way that is not constrained by the presently
existing system. In providing such a space, we are able to dream new
dreams, emptying ourselves of what we take for granted and allowing a new vision of the kingdom to be born. Instead of the naive
attempt to return to the early church (the church before Constantine
or before Platonic ideas or before Paul), suspended space is about
returning to the event that gave birth to the early church, providing a
space for that event to take hold once more and transform the world
we currently inhabit.

Once the supposedly immovable socio-symbolic system that
grounds our world is placed into question (the structure that defines
who is inside and who is outside, who is slave and who is free), we
can then imagine and enact strategies that will facilitate real change;
then we can allow the gospel to speak again in a new epoch. Why?
Because the first step to imagining substantive change (rather than
merely working within the current system) involves exposing the world
that we inhabit as contingent and not necessary, as something that
can be ruptured and reconfigured. The Christian community can then
imagine alternative possibilities and experiment with small insur-
rectionary spaces in which we live out a radical existence in fidelity
to the way of Christ.

By developing practices that help to form desert spaces within the
oasis of our lives, we can engage more productively in social trans-

formation. By having a space in our week where there is "neither/ nor," where we not only affirm one another in excess of our culturally given identities but expose these identities as contingent, we can more productively engage in exploring how to transform society.

Placing the hegemonic ideology of our age into question births collectives that break down what can seem like the most immovable social boundaries. Emmanuel Levinas beautifully summarized this encounter in an interview in which he commented that, if we see the color of someone's eyes, we are not relating to that person. One way of interpreting this is by noting that, if we are not really listening to someone, we will be well aware of the person's external features, such as the color of his eyes or the clothes she is wearing. However, once we get into a deep and intimate conversation, we will no longer notice these external features; we will no longer see the color of the person's eyes. It is not that they have become invisible to us but rather that we have entered into what Martin Buber has called an "I-Thou" relation, in which the objective nature of the other becomes invisible in the overwhelming visibility of the subjectivity of the other.

By forming a suspended space in which we participate in the divine kenosis, we allow for the possibility of encountering others beyond the categories that usually define them. We encounter the other beyond the color of his eyes, beyond the contours of her political and religious commitments.

What is noteworthy here is the idea that Christianity is not *fundamentally* hermeneutical but rather involves placing into question our various religious and political interpretations of reality. In other words, Christianity should not be approached as offering a thick interpretation of reality, an interpretation that would commit us to embracing a certain cosmology or anthropology. Rather, the fundamental Christian event involves exposing the contingency of all interpretations, opening up a desertlike space of negation where *metanoia* can take place (i.e., a substantive change in the individual rather than a mere quantitative improvement).

In this nonhermeneutical approach, identifying with Christ involves laying down identity. Such thinking challenges some of the basic coordinates of much contemporary Christianity, in which it is assumed that faith implies endorsing a worldview that may be compared and contrasted with other worldviews. From this perspective we cannot suspend our cosmological and anthropological ideas without losing something essential to our faith. On the hermeneutical or worldview way of seeing things, our "Christian" ways of looking at the world (e.g., our anthropologies, cosmologies, politics, etc.) have some divine legitimacy rather than being human, all too human, attempts to negotiate our world. In contrast, the idea of suspended space draws out the extent to which Christianity is concerned not with interpreting the world in a particular static manner but rather with opening up possibilities for transforming that world, always with the poor and oppressed in mind.

Religionless Christianity

Dietrich Bonhoeffer was a theologian who began to fundamentally critique the idea that Christianity provided a matrix of meaning through which to ground our everyday activity. In his famous compilation *Letters and Papers from Prison*, we encounter some of Bonhoeffer's most intriguing and pregnant reflections concerning the future of Christianity. This work brings together various reflections he wrote while incarcerated in Tegel prison in Berlin at the close of the Second World War for his part in an assassination attempt against Hitler. The work itself can be compared to Pascal's *Pensées* inasmuch as it offers a stunning fragment of thought that bears witness to a larger vision that was never elaborated by the author.

One of the more interesting and intriguing ideas found in these fragments relates to what Bonhoeffer calls "religionless Christianity." For Bonhoeffer religion is only contingently related to Christianity. It is but one way that Christianity can manifest itself, a manifestation that is being increasingly exposed as inessential and problematic.

In order to understand what he means, we must first grasp how he defines the word *religion*. I am not interested here in carefully piecing together Bonhoeffer's developing view of religion over his wider body of work but instead am concerned only with what we find in his later work. For the later Bonhoeffer, religion describes the act of grounding our human story in some metaphysical entity.[1] In this way, his definition of religion is close to Heidegger's understanding of much scholastic theology as fundamentally onto-theo-logical,[2] a term derived from "Onto-theology," Heidegger's name for a theology that speaks of God in metaphysical terms, that is, as the guarantor of meaning.

Bonhoeffer understood that a metaphysical conception of God makes sense in certain contexts. For example, historically speaking, humans have by and large existed in a state of unknowing concerning the mechanisms of nature. In such a state it is quite natural to claim supernatural justifications for what we witness in the world, from the changing of the seasons to disease, famine, chance encounters, birth, and death.

However, since the intellectual advancements that gave rise to the Enlightenment, humanity has developed powerful tools with which to understand natural phenomena in natural terms. It is not that supernatural explanations have been disproved as such, but rather such prescientific explanations have ceased to serve any productive function; they have become increasingly superfluous or even counterproductive. The result is a God continually pushed to the edges of life, to a realm just beyond the horizon of our understanding. By thinking of God in this way, the believer has been increasingly faced with the sense that God is becoming less and less relevant to life. For every time our scientific understanding has advanced, the realm of God has diminished. This God who inhabits the gaps in our empirical knowledge thus seems to be in perpetual retreat.

While God was once employed to explain a whole spectrum of phenomena, in the modern world God became increasingly unnecessary as an explanation. Soon we find God brought into discourse only as an explanation for why anything exists at all.

For Bonhoeffer it is not that people necessarily stopped believing in this God but rather that God as an explanation has become less and less important. In a world where there is constant uncertainty and danger, one may well find great comfort in the belief that there is a loving, all-powerful being above us who is looking after our needs. However, as technology develops and human life becomes more stable, this God becomes less important. God's role as deus ex machina (i.e., an idea lowered into human discourse to give meaning to an inexplicable situation) has been gradually eroded. For instance, Bonhoeffer writes,

> Religious people speak of God when human knowledge (perhaps because they are too lazy to think) has come to an end, or when human resources fail—in fact it is always the *deus ex machina* that they bring on to the scene, either for the apparent solution of insoluble problems, or as strength in human failure—always, that is to say, exploring human weakness or human boundaries. Of necessity, that will go on only till people can by their own strength push these boundaries somewhat further out, so that God becomes superfluous as *deus ex machina*. I've come to be doubtful of talking about any human boundaries (is even death, which people now hardly fear, and is sin, which they now hardly understand, still a genuine boundary today?).[3]

The important insight here is found not in Bonhoeffer's more sociological predictions that the religious instinct will increasingly diminish but rather in his theological reflections on how God has historically been made manifest in Christianity as deus ex machina, a manifestation that, while understandable, can now be transcended.

The Death of God as Being

In Nietzsche, or rather Heidegger's influential reading of Nietzsche, we witness one of the most potent critiques of God as deus ex machina. Heidegger's somewhat Kierkegaardian reading of Nietzsche interprets his famous death-of-God parable as a direct attack on this onto-theo-logical conception of God rather than as a blanket attack on Christianity in general. It is here, in Heidegger's interpretation of Nietzsche, that we find a rejection of what Pascal called the God of the philosophers. Hence, in "The Word of Nietzsche: 'God Is Dead,'" Heidegger claims that

> Nietzsche does not consider the Christian life that existed once for a short space of time before the writing down of the Gospels and before the missionary propaganda of Paul to belong to Christendom. Christendom for Nietzsche is the historical, world-political phenomenon of the Church and its claim to power within the shaping of Western

humanity and its modern culture. Christendom in this sense and the Christianity of the New Testament are not the same.[4]

He argues that Nietzsche's "confrontation with Christendom is absolutely not in any way an attack against what is Christian any more than a critique of theology is necessarily a critique of faith."[5] Nietzsche's writing on the death of God, he notes, is rather a visceral way of heralding the end of a particular way of thinking about God.

This can be seen most clearly in *Twilight of the Idols*, where Nietzsche works through six conceptual phases that culminate in the abolition of the real world.[6] The first three stages detail the various ways in which the relationships between appearance and reality have traditionally been conceived. The first, broadly Platonic perspective conceives of a real that only the wise, the pious, and the virtuous can attain. The second, drawing on a culturally Christian notion, details a deferment between the apparent and the real, declaring that the real world is presently unattainable but possesses an eschatological dimension inasmuch as it is promised to the wise, the pious, and the virtuous. The third stage signals an ever-increasing distance between the real and the apparent, a move reminiscent of Kant, who writes of the thing-in-itself as totally unattainable, beyond even the promise yet still having a ghostly presence, offering consolation, demanding duty, and justifying ethical imperatives. Each of these stages refers to the real while simultaneously signaling its gradual retreat.

Then comes the fourth stage, in which the real is utterly unattainable and thus unknown. It offers no real consolation, redemption, or call to duty. Fifth, the real world is "an idea grown useless, superfluous, consequently a refuted idea: let us abolish it." Finally, the most pro-gressive stage is unveiled (the "mid-day" and "zenith of mankind"): here the real world is abolished. As a result Nietzsche writes, "What world is left? The apparent world perhaps? . . . But no! *With the real world we have also abolished the apparent world!*"[7] For Nietzsche this death of God thus refers, first and foremost, to the demise of the suprasensory realm and the downfall of the myth of the Platonic Real.

In this way Nietzsche's reflections on the death of God can be viewed as a critique of any definition of God in which the divine is reduced to an external idea employed to ground human experience.

This is not a classical philosophical argument that God, as a being, does not exist, but rather a more genealogical claim that this idea of God is becoming less and less important in people's daily lives. God may still be on the lips of some people when they are faced with a problem that human technology cannot yet fix, but God is not at the center of human experience. With the potent mix of thinkers like Feuerbach, Marx, and Freud, who explored metaphysical beliefs as projections of our fears, desires, and hopes, and alongside scientists who demonstrated that the various processes in the world could be explained without reference to any outside agent, God, as metaphysically conceived, has become little more than a word we use to describe the source of the universe.

This reading of Nietzsche as attacking a specific conception of God has had considerable impact on twentieth-century theology. Graham Ward notes that

> when Nietzsche makes the claim "God is dead" . . . it is not a theo-logical claim as it is in Hegel where the death of God is the death of Jesus Christ. . . . Neither is Nietzsche making the claim that "God does not exist"—an onto-theological claim made by an atheist. "God" in Nietzsche's assertion is used metonymically. That is, it is a name which substitutes for and sums up a way of doing philosophy in which a highest principle is sought that grounds the possibility of all things.[8]

Ward goes on to note that the term *God* in Nietzsche operates as a metonym for "absolute truth," "absolute goodness," "absolute reality," and "absolute reason"—in other words, God is another way of saying *being*.

Toward a God We Can Dance Before

Whatever the most appropriate interpretation of Nietzsche's procla-mation of God's death, Heidegger employs it to derive certain con-ceptual tools that allow him to perceive a Christian spirituality not constrained by onto-theo-logy, a Christianity that would affirm God without need of metaphysical categories. Instead he seeks to rediscover those parts of the New Testament that emphasize lived experience and to recover what he believes to be the original categories of Christian life. In a statement with strong Augustinian overtones, he writes,

> Theology is seeking a more primordial interpretation of man's Being toward God, prescribed by the meaning of faith itself and remaining within it. It is slowly beginning to understand once more Luther's insight that the "foundation" on which its system of dogma rests has not arisen from an inquiry in which faith is primary, and that conceptually this "foundation" not only is inadequate for the problematic of theology but conceals and distorts it.[9]

As such he encourages theologians to consider why they would ever want to rely on an epistemological edifice that is metaphysically grounded, either to speak of God or to argue for his existence—especially when the Judeo-Christian Scriptures openly testify to a relation with God rooted in something that is given to theology not as an object to be studied but rather as a reality to participate in.

In short, Heidegger joins with Pascal in his attack on the "God of the philosophers and scholars." Hence his comment that "before the *causa sui*, man can neither fall to his knees in awe nor can he play music and dance before this god."[10]

While Heidegger appears to oscillate between belief and unbelief, his rejection of God as *causa sui* is not some crude atheistic gesture. For this reason Heidegger believes that those who have experienced theology in its "very roots" would prefer to "remain silent about God when speaking in the realm of thinking,"[11] claiming that this "godless" thinking opens the way to an incoming of God that levels the idolatrous terrain of onto-theo-logy.

Living in the World as Living before God

Bonhoeffer was one of the few theologians of his day who really began to chart the theological consequences of such thinking, asking whether Christianity could manifest itself in a religionless manner, that is, in a manner that does not reduce God to a means of affirming some metaphysical view of reality. At one point he articulates this by writing, "The Pauline question whether circumcision is a condition of justification seems to me in present-day terms to be whether religion is a condition for salvation."[12]

For Bonhoeffer the rejection of religion means that one takes responsibility for one's own ideas and actions. Instead of justifying our ideas in relation to some absolute outside of existence, a religionless life is one in which we face up to the fact that we live fully in the world with no privileged occult knowledge. None of us is spared the difficult task of working through what ought to be done, no system can claim absolute legitimacy, and no one can ever sit back and think that his or her answers are somehow hardwired into the mind of God.

Instead of giving God a place (as an external third that grounds meaning), God is denied a place. People are encouraged to take responsibility for their own actions rather than trying to justify them in relation to some onto-theo-logical source. This means that we must take full responsibility for what we do and believe. However, as a dialectical thinker, Bonhoeffer does not stop with the humanist negation of the religious affirmation (which ultimately operates in the same conceptual register as the religious affirmation). In Bonhoeffer's work we witness the dialectical negation of negation, whereby the denial of a space for God becomes the means of affirming that God dwells in every place, not as one who started the universe but as one who is constantly remaking it through the works of those gathered in God's name.

This move negates the affirmation that God has a place (and as such occupies only one marginal location as an explanation) while also negating the negation that claims God has no place (we live as if there is no God, refusing metaphysical speculation as pointless) to draw out the Christian idea that God, for the believer, is to be uncovered in every place. Hence Bonhoeffer's dialectical claim, "We cannot be honest unless we recognize that we have to live in the world *etsi deus non daretur* [as if God did not exist]. And this is just what we do recognize—before God! God himself compels us to recognize it."[13] This is how we can approach the death and resurrection of Christ. God dies to us as the guarantor of meaning and is resurrected in the body of believers, in the places where two or three are gathered together in love, dedicated to the work of love. Here, in Christ, God as an otherworldly being that grounds the world in (metaphysical) meaning dies. This does not mean that there is no superior transcendence, that God as Creator does not exist. Rather it simply means that the privileged way of encountering and interacting with God is through loving the material world and those who dwell within it.

Christ in the World

We can see an expression of the idea that Christianity is this-worldly in the very logic of the incarnation itself. For here we read of God becoming one of us. With the incarnation, we do not find God in speculative thinking but rather in the life and work of a person. In the incarnation God enters the world in order to serve it, bringing healing and liberation to those who are poor and oppressed. For instance, this message is fundamental to understanding the theological depth of the claim to virgin birth. Around the time of Jesus, Caesar Augustus claimed to be born of a virgin, his way of claiming that his authority was divinely given and thus legitimate. And so when we read of Jesus's virgin birth, we must be sensitive to the political implications. Here the writers are presenting Jesus as one directly opposed to the power of Rome. We read that a new king has entered the world and a new kingdom is at hand. A kingdom not found in palaces and mansions but rather in stables and shacks. A kingdom not for the oppressors but for the oppressed, not for the ones with a voice but for those who are voiceless. A kingdom that directly challenges the power and authority of Rome with weakness and humility. The virgin birth can then be read as a protest narrative, a political narrative, a narrative that makes a this-worldly claim.

This incarnational narrative speaks not only of God's immersion in the world but also of the nature of that immersion. Jesus dwells with those who suffer, who are oppressed, who have been brought low by the powers and authorities. Jesus is born not in a mansion but in a manger. His kingdom exists for those who have been denied a place in the kingdoms of the world.

In the incarnation we encounter a kingdom of prejudice. This is not about bringing equality to all voices in society. Certain economic, social, and sexual locations are privileged in this kingdom. The issue of homosexuality, for instance, is not one in which we must fight for a gay person's right to be treated equally, to be accepted, and to have a voice. In an environment of homophobia, the voice of someone who is gay is not simply one voice among others that we must listen to. This voice represents the *privileged place*, the place where God speaks. This voice is not equal to every other voice; it is an avatar of God's voice; it becomes the site where we encounter the call of God. This particular voice, with its particular claims, momentarily becomes a universal message that calls for liberation on behalf of all those who are excluded.

Such thinking is explored in various emerging collectives. There is an implicit critique of God as deus ex machina and a concern with how Christianity has been reduced to a way of interpreting the world. Instead, emerging approaches to faith affirm the incarnation as a critique of the otherworldly conceptions of God and as showing us that, if we truly seek to be like God, then we must do as God did and become fully human. As Bonhoeffer writes, one must take "life in one's stride, with all its duties and problems, its successes and failures, its experiences and helplessness." It is only as we "participate in [God's] sufferings in the world and watch with Christ in Gethsemane" that we affirm Christianity. For "that is faith, that is *metanoia* and that is what makes a man and a Christian."[14]

Theology | Part 2

3

Consumer Liturgies and Their Corrosive Effects on Christian Identity

Jason Clark

Location, Location, Location

My initial location and engagement with the "emerging church" came from planting a church. Where I live on the edge of London, it seems that almost no one is connected to a local church of any kind, aside from Christmas and Easter events.[1] In our context we have found that it hasn't been enough to try to do church better—as if, in addressing the failings of the church with an improved church, we could somehow stem the tide of the loss of Christianity from our local community. Church is largely already gone from my locality, deracinated over the last few decades. Our question became not, how do we do church better so that people do not leave? but, how do we recover church for our context?

My second location for involvement in the emerging church is even more personal. In 1999, two years after our church plant had started, I left my work as an investment broker and financial planner in London and became a full-time pastor of our church community. With our small church planted, three children, and my wife, I celebrated my first day as a full-time minister and pastor by having a complete nervous breakdown.

Within that experience I hope my involvement with emerging church has not been an esoteric and exotic indulgence but rather something integral to processing the pain of finding a faith and a way of doing church that did not fit my own life, let alone the community we were trying to reach. So as a burned-out, hurting, pragmatic church planter, I did something I never thought I would do: I turned to the consolations of theological reflection with my questions.

As I tried to find people to ask for help with my questions, I quickly found myself in the company of a host of other church leaders from around the world, from seemingly every denomination, and none. We shared an experience of a world that had changed and for which the church had seemed ill prepared. That cluster of friends, conversations, gatherings, and resources eventually coalesced into what is now, for good and bad, generally called the "emerging church."

Now I find I am in a third location, that of looking back over a ten-year emerging-church journey. I have had the privilege of exploring with my church community a more holistic gospel, a deeper reengagement in social justice in our local community and internationally, the development of a creative arts community and a liturgical life, and the practice of environmental stewardship as integral to our faith. Alongside this we have explored doubt, mystery, and questions—the apophatic nature of Christian spirituality—around our ongoing, passionate, evangelical conviction of the reality of the death and resurrection of Jesus as the event that all of life should be ordered around, and our local community invited into.

Yet after that decade of theological reflection and exploration in my church community, I have been left more disquieted than ever. Why, with our best understandings of church as a mission to a post-Christian context, with all of the elements detailed above evident in the life of our church community, having seen our church grow significantly, why were so many of our friends, family, and local community still adopting a take-it-or-leave-it response to most interactions with our community and Christianity?

We have so many people experiencing love, care, support (financially, materially, relationally), and, within our charismatic identity, answers to prayer and experiences of Jesus intervening. Yet, after all this, there is all too often an almost existential shrug, as if to say, "That was nice," and then a turn to the real business of life, well away from any ongoing experience of Christianity, with us or with others. No amount of holistic, experiential, participatory, and culturally relevant interactions would lead people to consider that a suitable response was the handing over of their basis of reality to one that is found in Jesus, with other people.

I started to wonder if, in a secular and consumer society where people *think* of themselves as nonreligious, they are in fact *deeply* religious. I found myself asking: what if the people we interact with are so deeply embedded in a *religious* system that they are unable and unwilling to convert to Christianity as an alternative reality? Is there something about this alternative religious reality that co-opts and undermines our best missional interactions, rendering them powerless? What is the basis of that religious system? Is it consumerism and secularism? And if it is, how can we best understand and respond to it?

So for the rest of this chapter, I will explore some of the ways we've come to understand consumerism as a religious way of life as it relates to Christianity, and then I will conclude by examining a few of the key ways we have experienced the effects of this in how we do and are church. Let me be clear: I am not offering a judgment of the markets and consumerism as inherently corrupt and unhelpful. Rather, this essay is an exploration of where this particular Western dynamic and context might be causing problems for those of us trying to grow churches that lead to Christian identity and formation. A detailed analysis of capitalism, consumerism, and commodification is beyond the scope of this essay; however, as I go along I will note some of the detailed resources that substantiate the claims I make in this chapter.

Consumer Religion: Separation of Beliefs from Practice

Consumerism can be understood in many ways, but one way to start is by noting that it does not consist in a definable set of beliefs and ideologies that Christianity can counter. Rather, it is at heart a way of *relating to* beliefs. So often we think that if we identify the incorrect beliefs around us, we can counter them with the correct beliefs. Yet we live in a world that approaches belief for its own sake in a way that renders this approach ineffective. Consumer culture relates to beliefs as commodities to be used and marketed. Consumerism is not particularly interested in defending itself. In fact, you can criticize its beliefs as much as you want, because that will give it a marketing angle and some publicity. Dissent is so interwoven with the DNA of consumerism that capitalism uses any critique as raw materials for new consumer products.

It is not that there aren't beliefs embedded within consumerism that need challenging; rather, there is a deeper problem with consumerism, that of "commodification," which abstracts beliefs from concrete practices.[2] We say and think we believe things and then are unable to take any action based on those beliefs. It's not that our practices are inconsistent with our stated beliefs, however. For example, it's not that we say we want to shop ethically, while really we desire to spend the least amount possible for a product, regardless of how the product gets to us or how the company that brings it treats its workers. Rather, the very fact of commodification cuts us off from acting on our beliefs. As a result, the process of abstracting beliefs from contextual traditions weakens both their ability to influence concrete daily life and their connection to the communities within which they originate. As Vincent Miller describes it, there has been a shift "from a world in which beliefs held believers to one in which believers hold beliefs."[3] The result? "Traditions are pillaged for their symbolic content, which is then repackaged and recontextualized in ways that jettison their communal, ethical, and political consequence. Traditions are valued as sources of 'poetic and imaginative imagery,' while their logic, systems of doctrine, and rules of practice are dismissed for their rigidity and exclusivity."[4]

The machinery of advertising, consumerism's handmaiden, uses stolen symbols to promise experiences and ways of life, security, and transformation to the congregation of consumer culture.

The Privatization of Faith and Church

Another way to understand consumerism is to offer an "embodied imagination," a story for understanding human nature (anthropology) and human destiny (telos), a story that we organize our lives around. Consumerism answers the question, what is a good life? or, what is the good life? Its answer: living somewhere nice, living to a ripe old age, having certain life experiences before we die. And it offers to save us from the worst fate of all human fates: boredom.

Consumerism might best be understood as a *perverted* liturgy. Something we practice and embody with regular rituals. I look at the pressures on my teenage daughter, the expectations and self-enforced practices she subjects her body to in order to take part in the consumer-religion dream. Most demands of Christian life and practice seem to pale in comparison, especially in terms of the demands on our bodies, time, and energy. And if our bodies have been handed over to the logic and imagination of the market,[5] maybe our souls have been relinquished with them. With its demands on how we organize our lives, consumerism is a jealous god, not allowing our souls and bodies to be located in any other relationships, especially the body of Jesus, his church.

Recently my teenage daughter wrestled with taking part in a dance club on a Sunday that would require missing out on the regular worship life of our church community. Her dance teacher felt no restraint in "evangelizing" her, telling her that surely she could speak to God in private; why did she need church? Wouldn't church always be there in the future? Isn't the dance club what's really important? Her teacher, knowing that becoming a dancer requires learning the traditions of dance and regular practice with others, didn't realize that the logic of her argument extends to Christianity as a way of life. How often do we become captive to this consumer training and liturgy, organizing our lives around the consumer imagination of what life is really about, relegating Christianity and church to a mere supplement, a cultural accessory? Indeed, church has become nothing more than a meaningless expression of private religious association or a private club. But what if church were not just one choice among many but an ultimate and final choice?

A Battle of Wills

This process of abstraction and privatization "constructs every person as the author of his or her own identity and beliefs, expressed aesthetically through the consumption and display of commodities."[6] And within this creative expression of identity, the freedom of the individual is pitted against any organization or organized way of life with others.

Where once community and religious groups were a means to psychological health and human well-being, today consuming has replaced them. "People no longer hunger for salvation or an era of justice, but for 'the feeling, the momentary illusion, of personal well-being, health, and psychic security.'"[7] The commitment to self-made religious identity makes the maintenance of religious communities almost unsustainable. And those who synthesize their own religious beliefs still have the problem of connecting those beliefs to the warp and woof of everyday life—without a community to sustain them. Ironically, those able to maintain their own faith can only do so because of years of past training they had in church communities. Forming faith on one's own, without others, does not work. At least faith in anything other than self doesn't seem to work.

The consumer, self-creating, therapeutic individual goes hand in hand with modern marketing uses of religious symbols to construct and support our therapeutic choices. Within Christianity, however, the freedom of the individual and the community depend on each other. The Christian priority of solitude frees us from the oppression of communities, and communities free us from the oppression of individuality.[8] This contrasts with consumer society, where freedom is so often about the private liberation of self from the public, so that we might be dependent on no one. Perhaps we dream of winning the lottery so that we won't need to depend on anyone for anything and can purchase whatever we require.

Givenness: The Cost of Our Agency

For the self-creating individual in sole charge of his or her own identity and action, there seems to be nothing that is prior to "self." In this scheme no organization or institution provides givenness to human identity, only that which the self determines and orders within that organization. Where once school, hometown, family, and church gave shape to our identity, we now choose who we are, free from those communities. This isn't always a bad thing, and for me personally a market consumer system meant that I could pursue my Christian conversion and identity outside of the alcohol- and violence-filled environment of my domestic family.

Yet it seems that with respect to the church as organization and institution, there is no first-person possessive plural. Everything is "yours" or "mine"; there seems to be no "ours," no location of my identity as situated in a group of others. The "our" of institution and the plural of identity and being are missing.

Indeed, many ways of doing and being church seem to be about giving people the resources to continue making meaning of God on their own terms, isolated from others. But what if the nature of church is not a pragmatic and aesthetic free-for-all? What if there is a "givenness" to ecclesiology and church, a givenness in which we *find* our identity in contrast to the endless self-creation of identity of the modern consumer agent?

Is the church essentially instrumental, its identity being found in its function, or does it have an identity within creation that God himself has established?[9] The modern Western church has largely taken the view that the nature of church is instrumental, in that the church derives its identity from the mission of God's people in the world, where culture is the reality that forms the nature of church. Perhaps we see this in *The Shaping of Things to Come*, in which Alan Hirsch and Michael Frost describe ecclesiology as the most flexible of doctrines, that it is the person of Jesus at work in the context of mission and the reality of the world that determines the form and function of church.[10] Hirsch and Frost assert this so strongly that they claim we get things wrong if we "allow our notions of the church to qualify our sense of purpose and mission, [and] we can never be disciples of Jesus."[11]

I think that perhaps we need to reverse this thinking—that we need first to understand the nature of church, within the purposes of God, so that we can then understand the mission it has in the world, in forming the identity of Jesus with others. That understanding of the nature of church must come from a canonical understanding of the church in creation, traced through Scripture, as the fulfillment of God's purpose with Israel.[12] For too long we have understood Christian identity as a conversion to Christ with a later optional incorporation into the church. Or as Simon Chan describes it: "This is sometimes expressed in the concept of Mother Church, made famous by Cyprian: 'He who has not the Church for his Mother, has not God for his Father.' That is to say the church is our nourishing Mother, and we are entirely dependent on her for our existence as Christians."[13] Our fear of the suggestion that the church is required for Christian identity might reveal the depths of our consumer individualism. It's not that we have too high a view of church but too low and functional a view.

Perhaps the most audacious claim of Christianity in the modern world might be to suggest that human nature and the purpose of life are not self-creating and self-authenticating but find their rule, organization, and fulfillment in the humanity of Jesus Christ with others. We are not free to be whatever we want to be. Who we are is found in Jesus with others, the depths of which exceed anything we can be on our own. Yet, in trying to get at that givenness, we need to be reminded, on the one hand, that no "single institutional form or set of relations can claim finality of truthful expression of God's order" and, on the other hand, that church is not just whatever we want it to be, when we want it to be.[14]

What Caused All This?

Saint Augustine of Hippo suggested that, within the human condition, the root of our problems with the world and one another is that we have misdirected or redirected a natural desire for God toward mere things, sometimes even preferring desire itself to the only one who can ever satisfy our deepest desires. How many times have we wanted something only to be disappointed when it arrives? How often has the wanting itself been more enjoyable than the thing wanted? Overwhelmed by how much there is in the world, we collapse everything into ourselves. Our misplaced, misdirected desire reveals our deepest longings for transcendence, justice, and self-transformation. The result is that we become superficial, picking and choosing beliefs, shaping them around our particular practices. It's not that we shouldn't pick and choose in a changing world and form our faith in cultural context; after all, that's inherent to the nature of Christianity and mission. The problem is that, so often, we use the increasing resources available to us in increasingly shallow and superficial ways, ways lacking depth and absent attachment to anything other than how we feel.

Consumer Church and Ecclesiologies

If consumerism is understood as a religious way of life—a misdirected way perhaps, but religious nonetheless—how might this play out in the real world of mission and church life? What follows are a few suggestions that grew out of the experience of trying to plant and grow a church in a consumer context.

Blueprint Ecclesiologies

In our modern world we have the tendency to begin with a theory and then try to translate it into practice.[15] When something is not working, we theorize about why and then come up with another theoretical model and try to put *it* into action. We see this all too often within church contexts. We experience something about church that is not working, so we think, read, talk, discuss, idealize, blog, and suggest endlessly what church *should* be, and we give our new dreams of church creative names and then categorize them; but we just as often fail to make them concrete reality.

Having an ideal model for church allows us to talk about possibilities. We can propose a new model of church for our situation; we can suggest church reforms that would address the problems of the existing church. However, the day-to-day life of church remains at a distance from these hopes and dreams. It is as if there are two natures of church: the one we long and hope for, and the one we experience in the reality of everyday life.

So becomes the pattern. We continue to take a notion, a metaphor, be it "organic," "nodal," "hubbed," "real," "cell," or "emerging," and then we theorize about how church could make use of those metaphors. When we try to implement this new model of church in the real world, we find it still fails to do and be what we had hoped it would do and be. Then we move on to the next model. Maybe we then become depressed, cynical, and even more pathological in defining the church in terms of all the things we do not want it to be, as much as the things we want it to be. I just want to be part of a "real church," we might cry out in exasperation. Perhaps we have been part of real churches already but have simply failed to notice.

Models and theories can allow us to say helpful things (as we use them to map domains of our experience), but too often inherent in our ideas and models is an idealized notion of church. These idealized models are, unfortunately, separated from the reality of everyday church life. When our models force an agenda for changing our context in order to fit the model, something has gone wrong.

There is no single correct way of doing and being church. Trying not to be like other churches is, of course, just another conception and idealization, albeit a pathological one. While our prophetic visions of church should help us see where churches are not boasting solely in Jesus, they too often boast in themselves, and they justify their "correctness" by letting others know how they are not like "incorrect" models of church. Instead of the quest for a new, radical form of church, we might do well to understand the church in history, with all its flaws.

The Wellness of Church

In the world of psychiatry, students study not just the manifestations and causes of mental dysfunction but also the idea of "wellness," of what helps the well part of a patient become "more well," as it were. In the worlds of education and business, there is the move to explore and develop people's strengths rather than focus on their weaknesses. In considering developing countries, debt-relief agencies look for positive attributes in assessments instead of previous models that measured only bad ones.

This does not mean that we ignore glaring weaknesses and problems inherent to the system with which we are involved. What it does mean is that we stop focusing on what is wrong and start focusing on what is right.

I often wonder whether we have made a mistake in our assessments of church by becoming almost pathological. The various idealizations of church that we have only touched on here reach a terminus in complete pathology. We look at current forms of church, and church in the past, with an eye to the "ill health," its deformities, the things we dislike about it, and the like. We then construct idealizations of church in reaction to the sicknesses we diagnose. Church becomes about "not being," and we measure who we are by what the church does not do and what it isn't. We are left without any understanding of the "wellness" of the church at all.

In Europe, where the church has almost disappeared, this focus on what is wrong merely exacerbates the problem. It prevents us from viewing the people of God in a missional sense. We become pessimistic about church and in so doing shatter our confidence in church beyond restoration. Indeed, a pathological vision of church can become so bad that we begin to see ourselves as *post*church, *outside* and *beyond* church in order to escape the sickness that *is* church.

How do we avoid the slide into a pathological ecclesiology and understanding of church while attending to the very real problems of church? How do we speak prophetically, idealistically, and passionately to the need for church reformation while being practical and pragmatic, without losing confidence in change? How do we find the best of church through history, such that we are propelled forward into the future without, on the one hand, turning a blind eye to past failures or, on the other hand, fostering a negative and bilious cynicism that invalidates everything that has gone before us?

How can we arrive at a positive and enabling vision of church, one that leads to "wellness"? Perhaps we can start with a deeper understanding of church by valuing and affirming the many good things the Spirit has done in the past and is doing even now, in our own times, from the fluid and emerging forms of church situated outside existing church structures to "fresh expressions" of the inherited church as it experiments with new forms of church outside of tradition but in relationship to it. In both cases the focus ought to be on a deeper church, "deep church" if you will. Here the focus is not on what is wrong or invalid but rather on the challenge of being the church in the shared context we find ourselves in. Within deep church, there would be a project of recovery as opposed to rejection. Deep church would recover confidence in the gospel and Scripture, and it would access the spiritual resources of the historical church in nonsuperficial ways, such that we align ourselves with the work of the Holy Spirit in forming vibrant communities, living faithfully in discipleship to Jesus in our contemporary cultural context.

In deep church we would not simply repackage the past or become fashion victims of the emerging culture, but rather we would aspire to an understanding of church embedded in the past while also fully engaged in the present.

Institutional Imagination

Today there is a deep suspicion of organizations, hierarchy, and the nature of institutions as such. I am convinced that institutions are the enemy of good practice. Yet without institutions there is no good practice.[16] I mean by this that any institution that forms to deliver good practice will always wrestle with becoming so bureaucratic and concerned for itself that it undermines the very thing it seeks to deliver.

We see this today with hospitals, for example. Places dedicated to providing medical care to human beings can become so caught up in politics and management conflicts that the medical care they are supposed to provide is undermined and, in many cases, people suffer. We see the same with the church. The organization of the church to facilitate the incarnation of the gospel can quickly become an obstacle to incarnation. Often, in reaction to this reality, we come to think that having no programs, no hierarchy, and no institution at all will solve the problem. If the institution is getting in the way of the purpose, the reasoning goes, get rid of the institution. This response is so ingrained in us that the very word *institution* has become pejorative. What we need is not the absence of institutions but an articulate institutional imagination. If we get rid of hospitals, we might remove the problems they produce as institutions, but with them we also remove the provision of medical care from all who previously had access to it, or we restrict it to only a few who are in proximity to those who can provide it. The relevant issue is not whether we can avoid being an institution but that of imagining forms of institution that can support and not hinder the purposes for which they were created.[17] "Embodied patterns of witness that enable the transmission of the Christ Faith across generations require the building of institutions, that is, a stable structure of social interactions."[18]

Third Space and Other Social Imaginations

In terms of space, the places where church life takes place, there has also been a headlong rush into the "third space"[19] for church. This is the notion that between the home and workplace there is a neutral "third space" that people inhabit. It may be a café, a sports club, or what have you, a space in which we incarnate the church. Of course, incarnating mission into the spaces that people inhabit is one thing, but the complete reduction or relocation of church in that space panders to the worst of consumerism.

The idea of a neutral third space raises interesting questions. For example, Are these spaces really neutral? What takes place in them? What kind of human beings do they form? Take Starbucks, for example. It is not neutral. It costs money to be there, and it exists to produce profits for shareholders. In a world in which a place between the market and the state does not seem to exist—where the market has absorbed everything apart from the state—the church as a public body might just be the only place to stand apart from either. Or at least we might need to start asking what the church as an alternative to the space of the market might be able to offer.

Whether we adopt "third spaces" or some other metaphor, we might still ask: What is furnishing our "social imaginations"? What are we organizing our ways of life and church around? If we have rejected some of the trappings of modern church, such as the view that the church is a business run by CEOs, how do we evaluate new, emerging metaphors and avoid the unhappy discovery that they are formed just as unhelpfully around things other than Jesus?

Consider the fact that systems and organizational theory have latched onto things within nature as good examples of how to organize our ways of life. The book *The Starfish and the Spider*,[20] for example, espouses the nature of a starfish as a model for decentralized organizations. I have lost count of the number of blog and verbal references I have read and heard with regard to this picture of how we should do and be church. Yet, while the starfish is a good model and metaphor for forming some types of consumer business or al Qaeda terrorist cell groups,[21] we might worry whether they form human beings in the image of Jesus and his mission to redeem creation. At the very least, before adopting them we should consider whether these social imaginations further a christological reality and ordering of life (and church) around the resurrected Jesus.

So what might shape our imaginations instead of metaphors derived from social realities? Recently we have seen a turn to narrative theology, an understanding that theology finds its meaning within story rather than in mere propositional truths. More broadly, we learn and take part in life before God and with one another within story. It's not that story doesn't reveal "propositional truth"; rather, in terms of lived experience, story is what we primarily inhabit and live out of. We see this turn to narrative in the ubiquitous use of metaphors and imagination in emerging culture, like the images of starfish and the spiders as pictures of particular ecclesiologies. Although we have become attentive to the narrative of culture, we need a "canonical-linguistic" turn.[22] We need to let the story of *doctrine*, *Scripture*, and *church history* shape our imaginations and the grammar we use to narrate the Christian life rather than allowing the narrative to be limited solely by the grammar and imaginations of popular culture. There must be an interrelatedness between the story of our culture and the narrative of Scripture, an interplay between the two such that the gospel and mission of the church become incarnated in the warp and woof of popular culture without being diluted by popular culture.

Put another way, it's not enough that I encounter and make sense of my life in terms of the Christian story. The story of Jesus, of God's redemptive activity in and for the world, must become the story I find myself in.[23] My story must become located within the greater story of the Christian narrative, and my identity must move in unity with others. Moreover, the metaphors and story of Christianity must not only give shape to our reality but become our ultimate reality.[24] To the self-creating modern ear, that might sound like a loss of self and as such be regarded as untenable. If that is so, it reveals more about our isolated individualism than it does about Christian and cruciform identity with others. With this in mind, we can consider what kind of church leads to cruciform identity, to the unmasking and undoing of the myth of individualism that consumer liturgical formation produces; what kind of church leads instead to an exchange of stories, replacing fictions of self-creation with the true story of life lived *in* Jesus *with* others?

Real Revolution

I have suggested how consumer culture takes our dreams and desires for alternatives to the status quo, for change and revolution, and disengages them from any real and lasting concrete action. In their book *Rebel Sell*, Joseph Heath and Andrew Potter[25] provide one of the most compelling descriptions of this phenomenon by combining philosophical analysis of consumer culture with a review of popular culture. What they discover is that the popular notion of being "authentic" means being countercultural. And this often translates into the language of revolution, of trying to opt out of the system, to "jam" the prevailing culture. In practice, consumerism co-opts these impulses and uses them as raw material to repackage and sell.

This is how we consume church. We read books on missional church, attend missional events, leave existing churches to be revolutionary, and at the end of the day we end up "consuming" mission rather than doing the dirty work of bringing about a concrete church and mission. The process of consuming captures us—we consume the idea of our blueprint churches and ultimately do nothing in terms of real missions. The idea of the "trickster" as rebel, able to subvert the nature of church, is captive to the process of consumption. The rebel is not a rebel at all but rather is complicit in pandering to the agenda of consumerism. Saint Augustine warned of the danger of loving love itself, of misdirecting our affections as a means of escape into simulacra and simulation.[26] Likewise the love of revolution; the anticipation and excitement in being "rebellious" can and do pander to the titillation of consumer agency and result in no real revolution at all.

The "trickster" who seeks to subvert the church, to draw attention to the failings of the church, can end up as absurd as the man in a story from Immanuel Kant's lectures on anthropology who, on seeing a child fall into water and start to drown, complains that there is no one taking action to save the child.[27] I remember reading a well-known emerging-church blogger who wrote an autobiographical piece on why he had left his church. He described how the members of the church drove their cars past the poor, the homeless, and the drug addicted on their way to spending their money on holding a Sunday worship service, having bypassed the needs around them. It was enough for him, showing how the people of his church had failed to engage with the poor, to justify leaving his church. I wondered why the author was unable to stop on the way to the service, why he had not tried to minister and invite the other members of his community to serve the poor with him. Perhaps then something amazing and truly revolutionary could have taken place instead of his self-righteously leaving his church.

Private God Spaces and Worship Aesthetics

I have suggested that consumerist self-agency regards us as the sole creators of our lives, locating us prior to everything, including God. The result is that we end up with the private God space as the extension of our need to "consume" church. While we might have correctly critiqued the modern church as often being a "dispenser of religious goods and services," we are now in danger of continuing that process to its logical conclusion. We dispense our own religious goods by ourselves, to ourselves, within the shallow "bricolage" of consumerism and "commodification."

There is danger in forming solipsistic ecclesiologies or churches for one. The private God space can become a therapeutic location in which I am trapped trying to make sense of my Christian spirituality. Gone is the abandonment of myself in worship and service in response to who Jesus is and what he has done. The basis of solipsistic reality is playlist spirituality, downloaded on demand. And with an increasing tide of books devoted to the collapsing of church into the private God space, we must consider how we ever hope to construct a faith that forms us as Christians, with so many ways of doing church that have more in common with ways of forming us as isolated consumers.

Ironically, and as I mentioned earlier, some of the most ardent advocates and evangelists for "private God space" ecclesiologies are people who have been trained for extensive periods of time by the organized church in using the resources of the organized church to sustain themselves. While they might be able to gather people who are disaffected from church, the nature of their ongoing protest and desire to unmask what they see as wrong with church become unsustainable. I remember reading an article that, while seeking to reveal the consumer nature of church, went on to suggest a form of church that sounded as captive to consumerism as the one it left behind.[28] The author of that article boldly asks, "Does anyone ask whether the church is delivering what the market needs?" If anyone did, he might do what the author does, downloading talks by great speakers, listening to what he wants, when he wants, gathering resources without the control and inconvenience and costs of "organized" church. What the author seems not to realize is that the resources he is consuming come from organized and concrete communities that fund his consumer church habit. If everyone did what he did, there would be no resources from N. T. Wright or Rob Bell to download. And should the church be concerned with delivering what the market needs or wants anyway? How is this form of TiVo-iPod-Skype-plus-church any less harmful than the forms of church it seeks to get away from?

Too often, I fear, we end up "selling" one another the ecclesiological fictions of private God space, peddling idealized theories about church, armed with pathological descriptions of what is wrong but lacking any embodied or concrete missional and church life ourselves. I fear that some of the most vociferous voices calling for these kinds of emerging ecclesiologies are the further embodiment of consumer relationships. Telling others how the church should be, we can embody the ultimate expression of ecclesial solipsism, unable or unwilling to "smoke what we sell" back home. When presented with critiques and suggestions for how church should be, I often ask presenters if they can tell me how that looks back home in their local community and church life. The reply all too often is that there is no community back home, no home in which to live out their theories about how church should be done.

In no way do I mean to argue or suggest that the church is beyond critique; I hope I made that clear earlier. The church needs repeated and robust criticism. But the future of church is not to be found *outside* church, telling the church how and what it should be; the future of church resides with those who, though critical, are nonetheless devoted to living within it.

Conclusion: The Invitation to Deep Church

I set out in this essay to explore how consumerism functions analogously to a religious system, how it orders life and relationships, and the implications for our ecclesiology—the particular challenges this presents to communities seeking to coalesce around a cruciform identity and missional life.

Central to that exploration was examining how, despite claims to the contrary, consumerism has within it a particular understanding of human identity and the meaning and purpose of life, an understanding at odds with Christian identity and formation. In particular, consumerism often forms us into isolated individuals, driving us deeper into our fallen human condition of separation from God and one another (as well as opening up the most amazing possibilities for connection and collaboration). Without an understanding of consumerism as religion, with its demands on our time, energy, and money, we are in danger of continuing to produce new ways of doing church that support those perverted forms of identity rather than creating ones that lead to Christian identity. In that respect I wondered if we succeed in describing the problems of church but fail to articulate an imagination for church in our emerging culture that we can actually inhabit.

A cruciform and canonical imagination for church might provide just what is needed. The roots of a cruciform and canonical church go further than the hydroponic ecclesiologies of consumerism. A deeper church offers the opportunity to discover the ontology and givenness of church, to know that who I am is not just an individual in Christ but also a participant in the mission of the body of Jesus.

We have such an exalted view of the individual. What we need is to recover a high view of the church. At a time when the most "authentic" thing to do seems to be to abandon faith and leave church, we need to rediscover the implications for Christian identity of being an active part of a community. A deeper church offers an alternative to the relentless pressure of consumer liturgy, a liturgy endlessly constructing perverted self-images.

If the church is to have any future, other than as an optional club within consumerism, if it is to turn to conversion and Christian identity, we must recover the notion that ecclesiology, the nature of church itself, is "an intrinsic part of the doctrine of the Gospel of Jesus Christ, not an administrative arrangement for the sake of the Gospel of securing practical results."[29] We must understand the nature of church as the public of the Holy Spirit,[30] a way of life together, where the church *is* mission, *within* Christ *for* the world. We must recover together a confidence in confession of the Nicene-Constantinopolitan Creed and declare that "we believe in the one holy catholic and apostolic church."

In my other chapter in this volume, I explore a possible remedy to the effects of consumerism—that of the liturgical nature of life, and how we might counter the liturgies of consumerism with Christian practices in church communities.

4

Thy Kingdom Come (on Earth)

An Emerging Eschatology

KEVIN CORCORAN

In my previous contribution to this volume, I suggested that participants in the emerging conversation have a tendency to look askance at
something we called *philosophical realism*. There is another tendency,
however, that appears to me preeminent among emerging Christians,
and that is a deep conviction that *this* world provides the permanent
address of God's kingdom. Emerging folk are, it seems, an *eschatological* lot, people who seek to make God's future a *present* reality, as
best they can. They are not shy about it either. Nor are they a posse of
pessimists. In this chapter I sketch one way of understanding emerging
eschatology and the Christian vocation in light of it. In a later section
I briefly contrast this with an alternative interpretation of emerging
eschatology provided by John Caputo via Jacques Derrida, a view
that some emerging Christians find especially congenial to their own
postmodern sensibilities. I suggest that, while something valuable and

important may be gleaned from the Derrida-Caputo model, there is, in the end, something disturbingly and fundamentally *dis*carnational about it, and insofar as it is discarnational, although helpful in some ways, it ought ultimately to be rejected.

Eschatology as End Times

In some circles talk of eschatology is synonymous with talk of the rapture, that immanent event in human history when, it is believed, Jesus will descend from heaven and those believers still on the earth will be instantaneously snatched away—pilots from jumbo jets full of passengers, drivers from minivans and tractor trailers on crowded highways, loved ones from animated dinner conversation and warm beds—snatched away to meet Jesus in the air. Before the Left Behind series, back in the late 1960s, there was even a song expressing this chilling prospect by the father of Christian rock, the late Larry Norman. It was called "I Wish We'd All Been Ready." Here are some of the stirring lyrics to that song:

> a man and wife asleep in bed
> she hears a noise and turns her head
>   he's gone
> I wish we'd all been ready
>
> two men walking up a hill
> one disappears and one's left standing still
> I wish we'd all been ready[1]

For conservative Christians, the touchstone for thinking about eschatology is 1 Thessalonians 4:16–17 and Revelation 20. In 1 Thessalonians 4, Paul speaks of the Lord descending and the saints now living rising to meet him in the air along with the departed saints, while Revelation 20 speaks of the thousand-year reign of Christ and the simultaneous thousand-year binding of Satan.

From this perspective, discussion of eschatology centers around such issues as *premillennialism, amillennialism,* and *postmillennialism,* each concerned with the thousand-year reign of Christ on earth.

The premillennialists claim that the current age is an age *prior to* the thousand-year reign of Christ; the amillennialists *deny* a literal interpretation of Revelation 20 altogether, insisting that the reign of Christ has already begun; and the postmillennialists claim that the second coming of Christ occurs *after* the thousand-year earthly reign of Christ.

As you might imagine, defenses of pre-, a-, and postmillennialism fill volumes of theological treatises. And those volumes are, as you might also imagine, chock-full of careful argumentation and exacting detail. It's the sort of discussion that drives emerging Christians nuts, as the desire to nail down with absolute certainty permeates page after page. Emerging Christians have little interest in such projects. They tend to be practitioners and activists rather than theoreticians, big-picture dreamers and visionaries rather than logic choppers and minutiae mongers.

If you think that eschatology is concerned *only* with such topics as millennialism and rapture, then you're likely to think that emerging Christians have no interest in eschatology, given that they have little if any interest in these topics. But that would be a mistake, evidence of a Procrustean understanding of eschatology.

Eschatology

Our English word *eschatology* comes from the Greek *eschatos* (last) and *logia* (the study of, discourse about). Eschatology is concerned with end times, last things, the future, destiny, where things are headed, where things are going *in the end*. In this sense Christian eschatology is *teleological*; that is, the destiny of all things concerns the *end* of all things; not *end* in the sense of things *coming to an end* or demise but in the sense of things being directed toward a goal or purpose, the sense of things arriving at their destiny, reaching the end that God set for them in creation. It is in this sense of "last things" or "eschatology" that I want to suggest one way of understanding *emerging* eschatology.

A Kingdom Come and Still Coming

In one sense emerging Christians are extremely sanguine about reality, about culture, society, and the future, even if they are decidedly not *triumphalists*. They are not blind to hate, economic injustice, greed, exploitation, fear, war, poverty, racism, sexism, consumerism, intolerance, and the host of other ills that plague our communities, societies, and world, not to mention our own hearts. But emerging Christians believe that an alternative reality is possible. And when I say "possible," I mean not in some weak mathematical or logical sense but in a much more robust sense. Emerging Christians live as though they believe that this alternative reality is in an important sense *already* actual, that it is scattered about here and there, and they are anxious to find it, nurture it, and dwell within it.

Now many Christians, including the vast majority of students who fill my introductory-level philosophy courses, believe that we know very little, if anything, of what heaven will be like. Emerging Christians live as though they vehemently disagree. They live as though they believe that we have a very good idea of what heaven will look like. Take Psalm 72, for instance. It happens to be one of my favorite psalms. In it the psalmist anticipates a future king whose reign will bring about unparalleled human and terrestrial flourishing. Here is Psalm 72, in its entirety:

> Give the king thy justice, O God,
> > and thy righteousness to the royal son!
> May he judge thy people with righteousness,
> > and thy poor with justice!
> Let the mountains bear prosperity for the people,
> > and the hills, in righteousness!
> May he defend the cause of the poor of the people,
> > give deliverance to the needy,
> > and crush the oppressor!
>
> May he live while the sun endures,
> > and as long as the moon, throughout all generations!
> May he be like rain that falls on the mown grass,
> > like showers that water the earth!
> In his days may righteousness flourish,
> > and peace abound, till the moon be no more!

May he have dominion from sea to sea,
> and from the River to the ends of the earth!
May his foes bow down before him,
> and his enemies lick the dust!
May the kings of Tarshish and of the isles
> render him tribute,
may the kings of Sheba and Seba bring gifts!
May all kings fall down before him,
> all nations serve him!

For he delivers the needy when he calls,
> the poor and him who has no helper.
He has pity on the weak and the needy,
> and saves the lives of the needy.
From oppression and violence he redeems their life;
> and precious is their blood in his sight.

Long may he live,
> may gold of Sheba be given to him!
May prayer be made for him continually,
> and blessings invoked for him all the day!
May there be abundance of grain in the land;
> on the tops of the mountains may it wave;
> may its fruit be like Lebanon;
and may men blossom forth from the cities
> like the grass of the field!
May his name endure for ever,
> his fame continue as long as the sun!
May men bless themselves by him, all nations call him blessed!

Blessed be the LORD, the God of Israel,
> who alone does wondrous things.
Blessed be his glorious name for ever;
> may his glory fill the whole earth! Amen and Amen!

The prayers of David, the son of Jesse, are ended. (RSV)

This is a picture of heaven, of that space where God's rule is manifest, the new Jerusalem. Heaven was and still is a future. But Scripture passages like this suggest that heaven is not *up, up, and away*; and they surely do not picture heaven as a future reality in which one enjoys God in splendid isolation, oblivious to everyone and everything, save God. A biblical view of heaven suggests a radically social, cultural, carnal, and sensual reality, and it is out in front of us; it is a destiny toward which *all created things* are moving. In heaven, in that future, there will be abundance and prosperity. In that future the poor and needy will be delivered and defended. In that future righteousness will flourish, and God will be like the rain and we like the earth, like mown grass onto which God will rain down and shower. That future, that reality, is one well worth getting excited about, and emerging Christians are excited about it. It is *the* alternative reality.

Indeed, Jesus proclaims this kingdom reality. Consider Luke 4:16–21.

> When he came to Nazareth, where he had been brought up, he went to the synagogue on the sabbath day, as was his custom. He stood up to read, and the scroll of the prophet Isaiah was given to him. He unrolled the scroll and found the place where it was written:
>
>> "The Spirit of the Lord is upon me
>>   because he has anointed me
>>   to bring good news to the poor.
>> He has sent me to proclaim release to the captives
>>   and recovery of sight to the blind,
>>   to let the oppressed go free,
>> to proclaim the year of the Lord's favor."
>
> And he rolled up the scroll, gave it back to the attendant, and sat down. The eyes of all in the synagogue were fixed on him. Then he began to say to them, "Today this scripture has been fulfilled in your hearing."

In this alternative reality the blind are made to see, the lame to walk, and the deaf to hear. In this alternative reality people are healed and flourish. Consider Jesus again, walking about the streets of Galilee, announcing, "The kingdom of heaven is at hand," "The kingdom of God is at hand." And then what is it that Jesus does immediately upon announcing the present reality of this kingdom? He makes a blind man see or a lame man walk. It is as though Jesus is anticipating the question, "But Rabbi, what is this kingdom like?" and Jesus, in healing and making whole, provides a concrete picture. It's like *this*! In this new reality the blind see and the deaf hear. In this new reality sins are forgiven and people are made whole.

So heaven is a kingdom and kingdoms have kings. As a Christian, I believe that the king of kings is, in fact, Jesus from Nazareth. As a Christian, I believe that the king envisioned in Psalm 72 is, ultimately, Jesus and that his kingdom has come and been inaugurated. In a sense, therefore, the future is—as emerging Christians live as though they recognize—*now*. Heaven is *here* and *now*. In this view heaven is not a place where disembodied souls go after the bodies they animate die. Heaven is here, now, embodied in earth and mud. Granted, this kingdom has not yet been consummated or *fully* actualized. Still, it *is* here and it *is* now. It is a kingdom come and *still coming*.

Here? Now? A quick glance around our world reveals poverty amid plenty, and no small amount of wickedness, strife, and oppression of various and sundry sorts. Indeed, a healthy dose of reality is enough to make many of us pessimists and to apparently give the lie to Psalm 72 and to the claims I have been making about heaven as a present reality. So how is it that one can suggest that the kingdom *has come*, is *already* here? If it's here, why don't we see it?

As I've said, the kingdom has not yet been fully actualized or consummated. It is still a kingdom *on its way*, even if it is also, and at the same time, a kingdom *already come*. For those with eyes to see and ears to hear, there is actually ample evidence of its present reality. Indeed, signs and foretastes of its presence are everywhere. Wherever you witness the tender, pregnant embrace of reconciliation; glimpse the healing touch of forgiveness both given and received; notice small bands of people living cooperatively, sharing possessions, feeding the hungry, clothing the naked, loving the severely, profoundly mentally retarded, defending the cause of the poor, defending the proverbial widow, orphan, and alien—whoever they may be—there you are witness to the *present* reality of God's kingdom. Wherever you find people healing one another's wounds, praying and working for justice and peace, railing against injustice and oppression, wherever you discover broken lives made whole and redeemed, there you are witness to the present reality of God's kingdom. It is all around us.

And those with magic eyes, eyes and lives and hearts that have been opened, they see it.

Let me cite just a few concrete examples of this present reality. In northeast Philadelphia there is a community of ordinary radicals, led by Shane Claiborne and Steve Moffett. About ten years ago they moved into one of the poorest and most neglected neighborhoods in northeast Philadelphia. What they do there is incarnate the kingdom. They grow food for the neighborhood, fight city hall on behalf of the widow, orphan, and alien. Literally. They eat and drink with drug addicts, prostitutes, and the homeless. They irritate the authorities and practice hope for the downtrodden and disenfranchised. And they do it with a refreshing and disarming element of playfulness.

The Simple Way and Potter Street are fairly well known because of Shane Claiborne. But many ordinary radicals that you have never heard of and likely never will are sowing parables of heaven all across the land. The reason you've never heard of them is that because like God, who wrapped himself in human skin, they clothe themselves in the all too ordinary and so go largely unnoticed by the people around them, just like God in Christ. "Isn't that Joseph's and Mary's boy?" It's as though the people thought, "You mean to tell me that this little boy that we grew up with, played with, and have known all our lives is the Christ? Are you nuts?"

In my own adopted hometown of Grand Rapids, Michigan, there is a community known as the Stockbridge Boiler Room. Its members bought a two-story home in the lower west end of Grand Rapids. The neighborhood boasts a thriving drug trade and is home to more open Child Protective Service cases than any zip code (save one) in West Michigan. But there, in the midst of the down and out, a small group of people gather daily to dream together, pray together, love together, and eat together. Here is how one of the founders of the community describes it:

> We're part of a movement that refuses to believe God wasn't really serious when he told the rich man to sell his possessions and give them to the poor, so we're trying to do that.
>
> And, we're part of a movement that knows grace: we're addicts and adulterers and cheaters and gluttons and prideful and habitual liars.

We gossip. Sometimes we're too lazy and self-absorbed to get up and answer the door when Christ himself is knocking. We buy things we don't need, sometimes, extravagant things, because we think we're worth it.

And all those sins, and all that grace, are in the DNA of this army.[2]

I would add: an army of love, an army of grace, an army of hope. There are others too, people and communities all over our cities and towns—vigilantes of love, practitioners of resurrection, mercenaries of grace, quietly and powerfully making evident the present reality of heaven, of God's kingdom.

A Kingdom Not of This World

Some might wonder how the view I have been describing squares with the biblical teaching of Jesus, according to which his kingdom is *not of this world*. How can God's kingdom both be and not be of this world? The short answer is that it cannot be, at least not in the same sense. So there is a sense in which it is true to say that God's kingdom is *not* of this world and another perfectly good sense, a different sense, in which it is true to say that his kingdom *is* of this world. The key is to distinguish between those two senses.

The sense in which God's kingdom is very much of this world is the perfectly good and biblical sense that I have been describing, the sense in which we human beings have been made from the mud and dirt—God-blessed, God-loved, and God-embraced mud and dirt—and made for life in an equally earthy environment. It is the sense in which God's reconciling, redemptive, and restorative activity takes place within the natural, material world. This is the theater of God's redemptive activity, the theater of God's kingdom.

The sense in which God's kingdom is *not* of this world is the perfectly good and biblical sense in which it is true to say that God's ways are not the ways of the world. God's aims and intentions, the way God goes about God's business, run orthogonal to the ways the world goes about its business. Where the rhythms of the world beat with power, prestige, and pretension, the rhythms of God ring with humility, meekness, and compassion. Where the ways of the world exhaust us and leave us with a sense of emptiness and loneliness, the ways and works of God eventuate in rest, fullness, and community.

God's kingdom is of this world in the sense that this world is the space and theater of God's redemptive and restorative program; it tells us *where* God's kingdom is. It is where it all began and where it all will be consummated. God's kingdom is *not* of this world in the sense that the animating principles that govern God's kingdom are utterly foreign to the animating principles that govern the great kingdoms and empires of humans in open rebellion against God.

Emerging?

What, you may ask, is peculiarly *emerging* about the vision of the eschaton I have articulated? Is it not in the end a rather *old* view of last things? In one sense it is true that there is not much new here. In fact, I think that when so-called emerging Christians are at their best, they make no claims to originality. Instead, in good postmodern or deconstructive form, they help us, the church, recover ancient insights, listen to ancient voices too long ignored or overlooked. What *is* somewhat remarkable among emerging Christians, however, is the acknowledgment that flashes of God's kingdom are just as likely to be found among those who do not identify themselves with Christ as they are among those who do. And emerging Christians are comfortable and content to cooperate with anyone, anywhere, who is about the business of God's kingdom, regardless of religious persuasion or complete lack of religious sensibility. Emerging Christians are marked by a spirit of collaboration in their work for the new reality that is God's kingdom.

This, of course, raises the issue of religious pluralism. Are emerging Christians religious pluralists? That depends on what one means by *religious pluralism*. If one means that God is indiscriminately at work in the world, bringing about God's good purposes through human agents, regardless of religion or creed, then I suppose emerging Christians *are* religious pluralists, and proud of it. For the record, so am I. But it should be noted that religious pluralism in this sense is to be distinguished from religious pluralism in the sense that all religions offer not simply equal but also *salvific* access to God. Many of the emerging Christians I know believe that devout and sincere practitioners of religious traditions other than Christianity have genuine *experiences* of God, that God has not limited God's self-disclosure to Christians. But, again, this is not to deny that God was *uniquely* present in Jesus and that salvation comes through Christ alone. Indeed, most of the emerging Christians I have spoken with do in fact believe that God was uniquely present in Christ and that salvation comes through Christ and Christ alone.

I should hasten to point out that one might be an exclusivist in the sense of believing that God works salvation and reconciliation through Christ *alone* and an inclusivist or universalist with respect to whom that salvation and reconciliation ultimately applies. And, in fact, many in the emerging conversation find what I like to call *christocentric universalism*—the belief that eventually *all* human beings are reconciled to God in Christ—extremely attractive. Some, sadly, may first need to experience the torments of hell, but eventually love will win, God will win, and *all* will be saved.

An Alternative Eschatology

Some in the emerging conversation work with a very different view of eschatology, one owing to the philosophical work of French philosopher Jacques Derrida. John Caputo and Peter Rollins are two postmodern philosophers of religion who have developed the Derridean notion of the *perpetual deferral* of the kingdom of God. On this model, God's kingdom is ever coming but never arriving. I have discovered many in the emerging movement who find what I will call the Derrida-Caputo conception alluring and attractive. While I find that certain aspects of the view offer a helpful corrective to excessive confidence and brazen certainty in one's grasp of God's ends, I believe that ultimately the Derrida-Caputo model ought to be rejected. In fact, I wonder whether it might not actually be something other than the *eternal deferral* element that emerging types find appealing in the Derrida-Caputo model of eschatology and that they misidentify as the doctrine of eternal deferral.

Let me be clear here. I am no Derrida scholar. So I will begin this section by laying out what I understand to be the gist of the Derrida-Caputo model, paying special attention to their idea of the impossibility and undeconstructibility of the kingdom, and I will leave it to the experts to correct me if I fail to see things correctly.

As I understand it, the *kingdom of God* or *Justice* or the *Wholly Other* or *Messiah* (all used interchangeably by Derrida, near as I can tell) is never fully present on the Derrida-Caputo model but always a reality yet to come, always a reality beyond, a future, a hope, an aspiration. Indeed, God is to be thought of not as a being, an individual, but rather as an uncontainable, unconditional, undeconstructible *event* that is, as some who talk about such things put it, "astir" or "harbored" in the name "God."

Why is the kingdom *eternally* deferred? Because words and worldly structures are finite, contingent, particular, limited, deconstructible, and thus *inhospitable* abodes for the Wholly Other and the Undeconstructible. At best we are ever presented with "traces" of the event that is God, and these traces call us beyond and invite us into a transformed way of being in the world.

As I said, I am open to correction here, as I am admittedly outside my own areas of professional expertise. But to the extent that I have the Derrida-Caputo model right, I am inclined to regard this eschatological model as utterly *discarnational* and so utterly foreign to the *incarnational* kingdom of Christian faith. Whereas the Derrida-Caputo "gospel" regards the contingent, particular, and deconstructible with suspicion and as inhospitable to the Wholly Other or Messiah or Kingdom or Justice, the God of Christian faith embraces, dwells within, inhabits, incarnates himself precisely in the particular, deconstructible, and contingent. And far from "traces" of God within the particular, deconstructible, and contingent, the gospel suggests a fullness of presence in the skin and bones of Jesus from Nazareth.

I find it puzzling that emerging Christians, who otherwise value and prize embodiment, contingency, and particularity in their various facets, are attracted to a view that, if anything, eschews the contingent, particular, and embodied when it comes to the kingdom of God.

Moreover, while the idea of a transformative event is at the very heart of the gospel and appears at the very heart of an emerging understanding of the divine, the trinitarian God of Christian theism is not himself an event, unless only in some metaphorical sense, but rather a God in three persons. *Events*, strictly speaking, are not the right sort of things to have intentions, aims, loves. One cannot enter into a reciprocated relationship of love and joy with an event.

So what, then, do many in the emerging conversation find so appealing in the Derrida-Caputo notion of God's kingdom if it's not the eternal deferral and impossibility of the kingdom? What, in other words, might they mistake for the eternal deferral of the kingdom?

Perhaps what many find appealing in the Derrida-Caputo model is the perpetual deferral of understanding or grasping, the realization that, no matter what we come to understand of God and of his justice, the reality of God and of God's kingdom is inexhaustible; there is always more. I wonder, in other words, if what many find appealing is the idea that we ought never to be satisfied or settle for a particular theology or a particular political arrangement, for example, as the *final* theology or political arrangement, but that we ought always to be questing, wrestling, reaching, and searching, recognizing that all theologies, all social and political arrangements, are provisional and temporary. As I say, this aspect of the Derrida-Caputo model certainly provides a corrective to an overweening confidence that regards *this* theology or *this* social arrangement as final and ultimate. But such a deferral is a fact about us and not a fact about God's kingdom *never* arriving.

A kingdom always coming but never arriving hardly strikes me as attractive or as *good* news. Such news is about as "good" as the news delivered up in *Waiting for Godot*. At least in the case of the latter the two characters *believe* Godot *is* coming, though he never arrives. Not so in the Derrida-Caputo story. In that story God's kingdom is in fact *never* coming because it is an impossibility.

Conclusion

The nineteenth-century German philosopher Immanuel Kant once said, in his inimitable and characteristically incomprehensible way, that "concepts without percepts are empty; percepts without concepts are blind." Unpacking just what Kant meant by this would involve, for me, explaining the obscure by way of the nebulous. I mention it only to highlight a salient feature of God's kingdom, namely, that it is a kingdom characterized by both compassion and justice. Compassion without justice is socially inert; justice without compassion is relationally cold. Compassion without justice can heal and bind up wounds, but it cannot move or inspire us to fix what is broken in the world. Justice without compassion can repair the ripped fabrics of social institutions, but it cannot bind up the brokenhearted and link human beings to one another. In the theater of God's kingdom, there is both justice and compassion, the structural and the relational.

Emerging Christians are anchored in the here and now. But they strive to live here and now in light of the there and then. The "there," I have been suggesting, is really *here*, and the "then" is the consummation of all things, the future, when Christ returns and is all in all, his kingdom fully realized, when the mountains bring forth prosperity for the people, the cause of the poor and oppressed is defended, and justice and peace kiss. It is a beautiful vision, and scores of Christians are being captivated by it. That, I believe, is a good thing for the church. A very good thing.

Worship | Part 3

5

The Renewal of Liturgy in the Emerging Church

JASON CLARK

My chapter on consumerism was an attempt as a church planter and pastor to reflect theologically on the real-world challenge of consumerism to concrete church and mission. In this chapter I give some explicit examples of practices and real-world engagement with that challenge. If my first chapter described a pastor and church planter trying to engage theologically, this chapter is an attempt to put legs on that theological reflection by showing what it might look like in a real-world church context.

This chapter will be far more personal, insofar as it is based on the lived habitat of my missional church community. I offer here examples of concrete mission and action, mission and action that has led to conversion and to development in Christian identity among my church community. In other words, it is my attempt to show that I "smoke what I sell."

In my previous chapter I suggested the recovery of liturgy as a response to the disconnection of belief from practice. Without a recovery and understanding of liturgy we are in danger of a collapse of ecclesiology and church into solipsistic worship aesthetics and private God spaces. In this chapter I want to explore liturgical practices as a means of stabilizing Christian identity and formation. For Christian liturgy has the power to unmask consumer identity and reveal the religious nature of market practices within our churches. Moreover, the practice of Christian liturgy has the power to align and order all our other habits and practices within Christian identity.

I begin by describing the impact of liturgy within my own community and its possibilities within story before describing the nature of liturgical formation and its impact on Christian identity and formation. I conclude with an outline of a short-term catechism program that embodies both the theological hopes and liturgical aspirations set out in the rest of this chapter.

Liturgical Ironies

I came to the Christian faith at my local Baptist church by way of a fairly dramatic conversion experience at the age of seventeen. My family was non-Christian, and until I went to a church service one October morning in a school hall, I had little connection to church other than school Christmas services at our town center's main Anglican church.

The Baptist church of which I became a member was life giving and wonderful. Yet I quickly acquired the bias and antipathy that existed toward liturgy. At its most simplistic, this belief considered liturgy something "religious" and held that religion was the enemy of "authentic relationship with God."

From the Baptist church I moved on to planting churches that were even "lower" in their ecclesiology; here casual dress, modern music, and meetings in schools and pubs were all the rage. In these contexts liturgical practices were perceived as something that at best were irrelevant and at worst decidedly unhelpful to the task of mission.

Yet here I am, ten years after planting the church that I still lead, using liturgical daily prayers, observing the church calendar, and planning our Eucharist services for 2009. I have found these liturgical

activities to be utterly life giving, revitalizing to my own faith, and
key to the evangelistic growth and spiritual formation of my formally
"low-church" community.

A couple of years ago, I was sharing some of these experiences with
a worship leader from a large Anglican church, who as good worship
leaders do, asked me what good resources our church was using for
worship. I started to tell him about how we had found the idea of the
"church calendar" and that we had been using it as a resource for the
worship life of our church community. As I was talking, he visibly
paled and then finally blurted out, "But isn't that all rather religious?"
The incongruity of the Anglican priest's concern for the low-church
minister's use of liturgy, seeing its use as unhelpfully "religious," was
not lost on me.

So what had changed? Why should I, and it would seem a great
many other low-church evangelicals, be discovering and embracing
liturgical rituals in our church practices?[1] Let me try to explain.

We Are All Liturgical

We are all liturgical in that we all have formularies that organize our
lives around certain beliefs and practices. As I look back at the low-
church worship patterns that I experienced, I can see that they had
their own "informal" liturgies. Doing the same things, at the same
time, in prescribed, regular, and set ways was just as liturgical as the
explicit liturgies of my local Anglican church. We even joked that in
a vineyard church[2] the services were regularly the same: a welcome, a
worship time with the band, some notices, a conversational teaching
time, and then prayer for people in response. I followed that pattern
for nearly twenty years. I think that qualifies as a liturgy!

The way we worshiped, our prayer times, our code of dress, where
we met, the things we did and the things we did not do, all could be
thought of as liturgies. Many of us in low-church traditions are now
acknowledging that liturgy and ritual have always been a part of our
church life, no matter how we have tried to avoid it or think otherwise. And not just church life is liturgical. Think about how families
observe holidays such as Easter and Christmas. We do many of the

same things year after year in the same way. We have inherited many of our holiday practices from our parents and they from theirs. In repeating these practices we recall and remind ourselves of the past, and in so doing we prepare ourselves for the future. Moreover, we have ritualized practices for ordering our days and weeks. Mine starts with brewing fresh coffee when I get to my office, and this orients me to the rest of my day.

What many of us in low-church traditions are discovering, as I described in my previous chapter, is that liturgy, ritualized practices—*even the secular liturgies of consumer culture*—form us. In other words, not only are there *sacred* liturgies such as those found in churches high and low, but our increasingly secular, consumerist, materialistic culture has its own set of liturgical practices, which everyone, even Christians, engage in, whether they realize it or not.

Centering our lives on our own happiness has led us to observe the consumer calendar with its relentless advertising, its demands for total obedience, and the complicity of media. We pursue a successful life, an early retirement by the sea, and freedom from commitment to anything except our own happiness. Our weeks are organized around the consumer calendar, so much so that we are now seeing a rise in "leisure sickness"[3] as we spend every weekend traveling to somewhere else in order "to be." Our consumer society can demand our total obedience with our relationships and the choices about where we live and the jobs we take.

Underneath the thin veneer of consumer *freedom* are secular liturgies that shape us and mold us. Indeed, many of us are ensnared and in bondage to the consumer machine. Its liturgies are immensely successful in forming us into little consumers. They dehumanize us by making almost impossible a way of life that is essentially connected to others and to local communities. I betray my suburban location here, but on the edge of London, everyone seems to be just passing through, there merely as a base for holiday and weekend departures to somewhere else. How odd that for many Christians, when it comes to hopes and aspirations, ours are no different from those who are not Christians.

Recognizing these two facts—that all church structures are liturgical in nature and that the liturgies of consumer culture often have more formative effects on us than our Christian faith does—many of us are returning to Christian liturgy and ritual to shape us and mold us in the image of Christ. In other words, since we are liturgical creatures by nature and since consumerism has its own distinctive liturgies and soul-shaping practices, we must become aware of them and engage in distinctively Christian liturgies that shape and form us differently.

What are the elements of liturgical recovery? What might they look like in the context of concrete communities? That is what I hope to show in what follows.

Gospel Amnesia

I live in a pluralistic society where Christianity is one story among many, a story largely seen as discredited. Indeed, there is deep suspicion of anyone who claims that his or her story is the one true story. The only true story is the one that we make for ourselves. Since there are many "selves" making stories, there are many true stories—not one.

Our society has little memory of the Christian faith that birthed many of the institutions we rely on, such as health care and education. We even examine our most famous and treasured historical novels without reference to the Christian faith and environment that inspired them. Not only do we have a culture that knows very little of the Christian story but also Christians who have forgotten their story.[4] Walter Brueggemann coined the term "Gospel Amnesia" as a description of this phenomenon.[5]

Although we may have forgotten the Christian story, we remain, as humans, captivated by stories. We still read stories, and we still go to the movies in large numbers. Brian McLaren, who has had an enormous impact on the evangelical church in recent years, explores the importance of story in his book *The Story We Find Ourselves In*.[6] The Christian story is the one we must locate our own stories in.

So, in a culture that has a plurality of stories, where the Christian story has been largely forgotten, and the Christian church seems to be suffering from a sort of amnesia, how do we retell the Christian story in a compelling way, and how do we locate ourselves within it? These questions have become increasingly important in my own church, not only for new Christians but also for those of us who have been Christians for some time. Thinking about these questions has led me to consider what the church in its history has done to help people remember and retell the Christian story. One of the things we have discovered in my own community is the church calendar, a simple tool used in Christian communities throughout history that organizes the church year around the retelling of the life of Jesus.[7] The calendar offers a way to order our lives around a different reality than that of consumption. Infused with the liturgies and rituals of Christian tradition, the church calendar provides a structured way to retell the Christian story as a community, to locate our own life stories in the midst of the Christian story.

Identity

If we delve into the issue of consumer identity a little deeper, and with the help of people such as Vincent Miller, we find that there has been a shift "from a world in which beliefs held believers to one in which believers hold beliefs."[8] Miller describes how consumerism, and in particular *commodification*, leads us to a situation in which individuals become the sole authors of their identity through consuming cultural aesthetics. We are whatever we want to be. We make ourselves in an image of our own manufacture. Often the selves we create are shallow and superficial, as they are based on issues of taste, personal preference, or whatever makes us happy.

This culture has a hugely deleterious effect on the way we relate to others, and it also has consequences for those of us trying to form church communities. In such a culture, involvement in church community becomes largely a matter of whether I am bored, offended, or interested, whether my perceived needs are met the few times I show up. If life is centered on my shifting needs and tastes, how can church hope to engage in mission with others? Church communities must respond to this situation constructively. Many of us are finding that liturgical rituals are helpful ways of responding.

With liturgy there is an invitation to participate, repeat, and enact something together as a community, something that reminds us of who we are and what we are here for. What we participate in, repeat, and enact is the Christian story, a story to order our lives. Liturgy and ritual open up the possibility of reconnecting beliefs to their origins and to the people who held and practiced them generations ago. They connect us to the past, to the story, and shape us for life together in an alien world.

Reciting together the Apostles' Creed can function as an anchor in the storm of conflicting beliefs that swirl around and within me. I am regularly moved by the experience of reading a liturgical prayer or confession where the voices of individuals, including my own, take on the univocal voice of a community. In a world where we are used to hearing the sound of our own voice out loud or within an internal commentary, liturgy enables us to locate our voice in the midst of others, to find ourselves in the identity of others.

The Mundane and Ordinary

We live in a world that does not know what to do with the ordinary. In fact, we try to avoid the ordinary and are encouraged to do so by everything from hair products promising to update our hairstyle to celebrity hypnotists promising to help us escape the drudgery of the everyday and ordinary. Books and magazines explain how we can liberate ourselves from the shackles of our mundane and ordinary lives.

A successful life is anything but ordinary. Even Christians accept this. Marriage books proclaim ten guaranteed steps to acquiring the perfect marriage; books on prayer offer steps to the perfect prayer life, and books on church promise techniques that will deliver the perfect church. Yet at a time when so many of us have so much more in terms of prosperity, and more resources available than ever to help us transform our lives, we seem to be more unhappy than our predecessors.[9]

While God does bring occasional "mountaintop times," much of life is lived in the mundane and ordinary. So, in a world obsessed with avoiding the ordinary, where Christian spirituality is often held captive to that process, where the measure of Christian life is how exciting or stimulating the Christian life is, how do we find meaning and connection in the mundane?

Perhaps part of the answer can be found in the church calendar. Within the church calendar there are three main seasons: fasting (Advent and Lent), feasting (Christmas and Easter), and ordinary time, for most of the time in between. By ordering our lives around the church calendar in our worship as communities, we get to place the 24/7 demands of our world within a different reality, a reality that confers deep meaning and significance on the ordinary.

The church calendar introduces us to the pattern of fasting, reminding us that life is often about lack, absence, and the need for preparation and longing. It also incorporates feast days of celebration. The small number of days in feast seasons is an immediate counter to the consumerist push for every day to be a day of plenty. The overwhelming amount of time in the church calendar given over to the ordinary is a reminder that most of life is about being faithful in the mundane of everyday life.

The church calendar is not just about *seasons*. It is also about our *daily* lives, calling us to order our lives by working and by observing a Sabbath day each week. This is a day on which we are called to worship, to connect, reflect, and be with our communities of faith and families. The Sabbath, unfortunately for us, has been replaced with ecstatic shopping and leisure experiences. Intentionally ordering our lives, placing our time within a liturgical pattern, enables us to confirm and affirm that life is not about "the business cycle, the need for greater productivity, or the possibilities of technology."[10]

Spiritual Formation

For many Christians, spiritual formation conjures images of learning facts and information. We cannot imagine that spiritual formation has anything to do with the cultivation of truly human lives lived in community and engaged in the mission of God.

The recovery of liturgy has been for many of us an opening of the vaults and archives of church history to discover the riches available to us in our formation as people and churches, formation that goes beyond the learning of Christian "facts." Liturgical rediscovery has also resulted in an explosion of creative arts, of painting, poetry, and music. New media and audiovisual technologies have become the new stained-glass windows of many church communities. Instead of undermining the life of Christians and their communities, liturgical practices have had the opposite effect. They have been a doorway into depths of growth.

Many of us are finding that the plurality of our world and culture is enriched, informed, and expanded by a church that is diverse, rich, deep, and complex, inviting people to locate themselves alongside us and with us. Liturgy and ritual can form our lives around the reality of the universe that is the life of Jesus.

Flow: A Short-Term Catechism

Last, I want to recount a particular liturgical practice of my church community.[11] This practice seeks to embody our aspirations for liturgical formation in ways that are practical for members of our community.

"Flow" is the name given to a new short-term catechism available to our church members. Described as "taking a short-term mission into your own life," the aim of Flow is the liturgical stabilization and formation of Christian identity in the face of the liturgies and demands of consumer culture and formation.

Background to Flow

In the context of our church plant, our problem is not that people spend too much time in church; it is that they are likely to spend so little time with Christians that the development of Christian habits and practices are unlikely to take root, and they will spend most of their time at work and in social environments where non-Christian identities are formed and practiced.

The beginning of our short-term catechism is marked by the desire to help Christians engage with liturgical practices that result in habits for Christian formation and that attend to Christian identity in all aspects of life, home, work, and the market. When Christian formation is neglected, it is not the case that formation is not happening; rather, formation is happening, but not formation of a Christian sort.

Flow is an attempt for a short period of time to fit life around the Christian faith and the Christian faith around life.

Conceptions for Flow

In our community, we talk about Flow as a "short-term mission," and we seek to replicate that experience. But instead of leaving our location, the mission is into our own life and work, among our own family and friends. In our post-Christian context, we may not have to step outside our own front door to experience the need for mission. So we seek through our church to provide an experience of mission in our own lives.

When people go on a mission for an intense time to explore a new horizon, to gain new experiences in a compressed and focused way, they return changed and full of memories that will stay with them and shape them for a lifetime. Flow is designed to have the very same effect.

So for forty days we commit to fitting our life into our faith in a secular world that tells us to keep our faith private and fit it in when we have spare time. For six weeks we have the opportunity to turn that around, to say no to many things and opportunities in order to say yes to something even better. Flow is an opportunity to go public and let our family, friends, coworkers, and ourselves know that we are fitting our life around our faith.

Three Key Elements

There are three key elements that our Flow program is designed around.

Doing—Understanding the interaction between gifts, strengths, and how serving shapes and forms us is the first vital element of Flow. Flow engages in concrete action, based on the belief that we need to *serve* and *do* in order to grow.

Knowing—The second element of Flow seeks to deepen faith, deepening our understanding of what we believe and why. This involves far more than propositional learning; it involves engaging the cognitive as well as the affective, facilitating changes in how we think and how we live. The goal is an increased understanding and ownership of the Christian faith.

Some of us have an in-depth knowledge of our favorite sports team, its history, and the vital statistics of our favorite players. This element of Flow seeks to develop a knowledge of the history and identity of the Christian church. It seeks to uncover what distinguishes the church as a community from the other groups and communities we belong to.

Being—The third element consists in personal reflection, reflection on who we are, what's going on in our lives and our relationships, including our relationship with Jesus. Who are we in Jesus and who are we in relationship with others?

Flow is an attempt to bring these three elements—*knowing, doing,* and *being* together.

Flow in Practice

As a short-term mission, Flow is designed with daily and weekly practices that engage these three areas of doing, knowing, and being.

1. Time: Flow involves a six-week commitment. This is not so long as to be impossible and onerous, but it is long enough to enable us to shape the rest of our life around our faith.
2. Daily: Each day includes prayers (a large number of options for daily praying are given, such as the use of MP3s, online resources, and books), with the aim of ensuring that our day is shaped by the rhythm of prayer.
3. Weekly Serving: Participants in Flow commit to attend service each Sunday during the six-week course. They are required to serve every Sunday and to pray for people every Sunday. If people are not used to giving, they are asked to practice tithing, investing some of their money in the mission of the Christian life as a counter to how they might usually spend their money.
4. Weekly Celebrating: Participants in Flow meet over a meal together each week and are encouraged to invite others—to

luxuriate in each other's company and enjoy celebrating each other's lives and all that Jesus is doing in and with each of us.

5. Training/Coaching: During the six-week course, participants read books, listen to teaching materials, and meet with Flow team leaders for training, reflection, and ministry. On Sunday at lunchtime, participants meet together for food and training.

Outcomes

The goal of Flow is to develop Christian habits and practices that will, by the end of the course, have become a natural and regular part of our lives. We aim to emerge from Flow closer to God and possessing a better idea of how he has wired us and what he is calling us to.

We want our family, coworkers, and friends to see and understand that we are Christian, and we hope we will have ongoing opportunities to tell them about how our lives are shaped around Jesus. We desire to know and draw comfort and inspiration from our Christian beliefs and be able to connect these to all parts of our lives. We also hope that by the end of the course we will have laughed, cried, and celebrated faith and life with others, deeply and meaningfully.

Conclusion

Like so many other Christian communities, mine is developing in the employment of creative arts. We have audiovisual and liturgical teams who use music, videos, poetry readings, and drama to bring the ancient and the future together and to add to the resources of the liturgical life of our community.

Daily prayers take place online; they are downloaded to people's MP3 players or sent via text messages to cell phones. The practice of living with intentionality in the community in this time and place, without being dictated to by the liturgy of consumerism, is beginning to take place. For many of us, the Eucharist (or Communion or Lord's Supper) is central to our liturgical lives. We seek to live in light of the church calendar, allowing it to serve as a reminder that we are called to become like Jesus and to order our whole lives after him.

What is at stake is nothing less than the stabilization of Christian identity in the face of consumer identity formation. We want to be committed to Christian identity, conversion, and development within the life of a concrete church community committed to mission, a community that resists the privatization and isolation of consumer formation and avoids collapsing faith into "private God space" spirituality. We believe the church is a community of people who practice together and learn the story, language, and grammar of faith together. We accept the call to reorder the very fabric of our lives around the reality of Jesus rather than accommodating to and fitting our ways of doing church around the religion of consumerism.

6

Transformance Art

Reconfiguring the Social Self

PETER ROLLINS

The Ironic Stance

There is an old anecdote that speaks of a young minister sitting in her house one Sunday afternoon when she is disturbed by a frantic banging on the front door. Upon opening the door, she is confronted by a distraught member of her church. It is obvious that he is exhausted from running to her house and is barely able to hold back some tears.

"What's wrong?" asks the minister.

"Please, can you help?" replies the man. "A kind and considerate family in the area is in great trouble. The husband recently lost his job, and the wife can't work due to health problems. They have three young children to look after, and the man's mother lives with them as she is unwell and needs constant care. They have no money at the moment, and if they don't pay the rent by tomorrow morning the landlord is going to kick them all onto the street, even though it's the middle of winter."

"That's terrible," says the minister. "Of course we will help. I will go get some money from the church fund to pay their rent. Anyway, how do you know them?"

"Oh," replies the man, "I'm the landlord!"

This story gains its power from the seemingly ridiculous gap that exists between the landlord's desire to help the family and the fact that it is his very actions that are causing the problem in the first place. Yet the humor of the story does not arise from the fact that there exists a gap between the landlord's intellectual desire to help the family and his social practice. Rather, it is created by the fact that the landlord does not experience this gap as a conflict at all. Indeed, it would not be unusual to find someone struggling between the values and the exigencies of modern life. There are no doubt many landlords who are faced with problems similar to the one above and who find themselves wrestling with the tension created by a longing to help those who are in need and the desire to remain financially secure. This story works as a joke because of the way in which the landlord does not face such an inner wrestling. He is perfectly able to both care deeply for the dire situation that the family faces while simultaneously being a prime influence in the creation of that situation. As such he is able to continue gaining his pleasure from being a landlord (making money off the family) while disavowing the pleasure so as to minimize any guilt.

While it is easy to dismiss the inconsistency generated by this story as an amusing fiction, a more careful reflection on our own lives may expose a similar and similarly disturbing gap. Does this story not express the ironic stance that is almost ubiquitous today? The ironic stance can be described as a way of distancing oneself from a certain social activity while simultaneously engaging in it. For instance, let us reflect on the popularity of parties in which those who attend are invited to dress up in the fashion of the seventies or eighties and dance to the most idiosyncratic and extreme music of the particular era. Here people are able to engage in an activity while intellectually distancing themselves from it: laughing at the music and the outfits while simultaneously dancing to the music and wearing the outfits. Thus one is able to ridicule the very activity that one is fully immersed in.

Consider: if you asked me whether I believed that owning my own home would make me happier or having a better car would make me feel more important or whether investing money would be something worth spending time and energy on, I would laugh and say, "Of course not." But place me in a position in which I was faced with one of these prospects, and I may well act as if I did believe. Most of us are concerned about ecological issues. We may talk about them a lot with our friends in some big coffee-chain café and think about them a lot as we drive about in our big car on the way to the shops to buy goods we do not need. We thus disavow the very activity we are engaged in. Indeed, we can even have faith gatherings exploring the issues and participate in some protests while not reconfiguring our social existence.

This ironic stance then does not refer to those who experience the gap between belief and action as one riven with conflict. Rather, like the landlord in the opening anecdote, it is manifest in the way that many of us can maintain a difference between our belief and practice so that it is not experienced as a conflict at all. Of course, some may feel that they do not have any significant gap between their beliefs and their actions. However, this is not necessarily a good thing. For many there is no disparity between their value system and their actions because their value system is dictated by whatever action brings most pleasure. We must not forget Nietzsche's lament concerning the lack of hypocrites in the world, a hypocrite being someone who lays claim to some values yet fails to live up to them. So many who decry hypocrisy today are not capable of reaching the level of hypocrisy. They simply embrace the values that they find easiest to maintain, the ones that justify their acts. It is not difficult to avoid hypocrisy when you believe in nothing. It is much harder when you believe in such things as simplicity, not exploiting workers through consumption, living with the oppressed, and giving in a sacrificial manner.

While the ironic gesture could be described as the ubiquitous stance of the cultured elite, it is easy to expose its impotency as a political and religious stance. For it allows one to disavow an activity as wrong in the very moment of engaging in that activity, deriving one's pleasure from an action while simultaneously critiquing it.

Perverse Transgression

This ironic stance can be maintained through engaging in what we may call *perverse transgression*. A perverse transgression is any act that appears to undermine a particular system but that actually affirms the very system it purports to attack.

A prime example of this can be found in the figure of Bruce Wayne. In each of the Batman films, Bruce is obsessed with stamping out street violence, an obsession that arises as a direct result of witnessing his mother and father murdered by a thief. His father was a philanthropist who attempted to help transform Gotham City by funding social projects and engaging in charitable activity. Bruce, however, takes a different approach and uses his wealth to fund a vigilante war on terror.

One could say that Bruce Wayne is fundamentally different from his father inasmuch as his father concentrated on helping victims of crime while Bruce seeks to punish the perpetrators of crime. However, it would be more accurate to say that Bruce is merely continuing his father's business by different, but equally flawed, means. Both are obsessed with the subjective violent eruptions that take place on the streets of Gotham City, and both seek to address them. However, in the midst of all their activities, neither pays attention to his own (sublimated) violence, a violence that has been objectified in the very economic structures that enable corporations like Wayne Industries to make such vast sums of money in the first place, amounts so monumental that Bruce can fund a large-scale, technologically advanced, clandestine military campaign without raising suspicions within the corporation itself. Bruce is unable to see that the subjective crime he fights on a nightly basis is the direct manifestation of the objective crime he perpetrates on a daily basis. The street crime he fights against is the direct explosion of violence that results from large, greedy industries obsessed with the increase of abstract capital at the expense of all else.

It is not enough to hate subjective explosions of crime; one must turn one's attention to what causes them. It is easy to find Christians during the time of slavery who argued that we must care for slaves and treat them with respect. However, what was needed at that time was courageous individuals such as William Wilberforce, who would question the objective conditions that sustained and maintained systems of slavery in the first place. It is one thing to give to the poor and another to do something about the conditions that create and sustain poverty.

The problem with Bruce Wayne is not simply that he fights street crime while failing to ask how it is sustained at a systemic level; rather, he fails to recognize that it is his daily activity that generates the crime he is attempting to fight. Of course, his main enemies are presented as having little interest in money, and there will always be some people who simply like to steal. But the greed of massive corporations and the poverty they create give oxygen to the fire of their evil schemes, creating the conditions for the proliferation of crime. Batman's archvillains would have a difficult time carrying out their crimes if they did not have a seemingly unlimited number of poor and desperate criminals supporting them.

For Bruce Wayne, his nightly attempts to change the heart of Gotham City are the very things that prevent him from creating real change. Why? Because he works hard by day to make vast sums of money so he can continue his campaign by night. He can feel good about himself, as some of the profit he makes goes to maintaining his nefarious activities.

In this way the very philanthropic work of his father and the crime fighting of Bruce actually provide the valve that allows them to continue contributing to a system of inequality that generates the very problems they are attempting to solve.

Perverse Transgression within the Church

Continuing in the tradition of Marx, Freud, and Nietzsche, Slavoj Žižek masterfully exposes how seemingly innocuous or benevolent acts can operate as a means of sustaining obscene desires. One example he uses relates to the increase of Buddhist practices in the West. In *On Belief* he writes,

> Western Buddhism . . . enables you to fully participate in the frantic pace of the Capitalist game while sustaining the belief that you are not really in it, that you are well aware of how worthless the spectacle

is—what really matters is the peace of the inner Self to which you
know you can always withdraw . . . as in the case of a Western Buddhist unaware that the "truth" or his existence is the social involvement
which he tends to dismiss as a mere game.[1]

Thus, elsewhere he is able to claim that "this pop-cultural phenomenon preaching inner distance and indifference toward the frantic pace
of market competition" used among businesspeople "is arguably the
most efficient way for us to fully participate in Capitalist dynamics
while retaining the appearance of mental sanity."[2] One of the ways
Western Buddhism does this is through its celebration of flux, change,
and the need to hold things lightly, all valuable techniques in the
business world, where stocks are in constant flux, people change jobs
regularly, and a wealthy person one day may find his or her invest-
ments have become worthless the next. The practice thus acts as a
lie that allows us to cope with the unbearable truth of our situation.

The question we must face in light of this reality concerns the extent
to which church activities themselves can act as a means of actually
encouraging the very ideology they appear to question. For instance,
is it possible that one way a person may be able to work tirelessly
in a job with questionable ethical practices (e.g., banks that invest
money in arms or jewelers that trade in blood diamonds) is because
they attend church once a week and volunteer at the local homeless
shelter on a Thursday evening? Such activities provide the individual
with a space to switch off their daily practices, recharge, and even
gain skills that enable their full immersion in the capitalist system. In
this perverse activity, individuals believe that what they are doing on
a Sunday morning and a Thursday evening defines their inner truth;
it is who they really are.

To what extent can our prayer meetings and weekly commitment
to the poor actually be the very activities that enable us to engage
in careers that help to perpetuate what we are praying against? Such
activities are perverse inasmuch as they recharge our batteries and
help us feel that our true identity is pure and good, when in reality
they simply remove the guilt that would otherwise make it difficult for
us to embrace our true (social) self, the self expressed in the activities
we engage in the rest of the week. What we are doing is really just

rearranging chairs on the *Titanic*. Our activities are radically displaced and thus indirectly contribute to what they directly disavow.

We know the world has problems, we know that we are in a difficult situation, and so on, but as long as we go to church on Sunday, meditation class on Thursday, and the local charity shop on Saturday, we don't have to face up to the objective violence of our daily life.

If this is the case, then a step in the right direction would involve cutting against one's very social activity, refusing the subjective supplement that allows us to continue to engage in an unjust economic system. Let us approach this logic via a parable.

There was once a fiery preacher who possessed a powerful but unusual gift. He found that, from an early age, when he prayed for individuals, they would supernaturally lose all of their religious convictions. When he prayed for people, they would invariably lose all of their beliefs about the prophets, the sacred Scriptures, and even God. As such he learned not to pray for people and instead to limit himself to inspiring sermons and good works.

However, one day, while traveling across the country, he found himself in conversation with a businessman who happened to be going in the same direction. This businessman was a very powerful and ruthless merchant banker, honored by his colleagues and respected by his adversaries.

Their conversation began because the businessman possessed a deep abiding faith and had noticed the preacher reading from the Bible. He introduced himself to the preacher, and they began to talk. As they chatted together, this powerful man told the preacher all about his faith in God and his love of Christ. He spoke of how his work did not really define who he was.

"The world of business is a cold one," he confided to the preacher, "and in my line of work there are situations I find myself in that challenge my Christian convictions. But I try, as much as possible, to remain true to my faith. Indeed, it is my faith that stops me from getting too caught up in that heartless world of work. So as not to get lost in this often heartless line of work, I attend a local church, participate in a prayer group, and contribute to a weekly Bible study. These activities help remind me of who I really am."

After listening carefully to the businessman's story, the preacher began to realize the purpose of his unseemly gift. And so he asked if he could pray for the businessman. The businessman readily agreed, unaware of what would happen. And sure enough, after the preacher had muttered a simple blessing, the man opened his eyes in astonishment.

"What a fool I have been for all these years!" he proclaimed. "It is clear to me now that there is no God above who is looking out for me, that there are no sacred texts to guide me, that there is no spirit to inspire and protect me."

As they parted company, the businessman, still confused by what had taken place, returned home. But now that he no longer had any religious beliefs left, he found it increasingly difficult to continue in his line of work. Faced with the fact that he was now just a hard-nosed businessman working in a corrupt system rather than a man of God, he began to despise himself. Within months he had a breakdown and gave up his line of work completely. Feeling better about himself, he then went on to give away the money he had accumulated to the poor and started to use his considerable managerial expertise challenging the very system he once participated in and helping those who had been oppressed by it.

One day, many years later, he happened upon the preacher again while walking through town. He ran up to him, fell at his feet, and began to weep with joy. Eventually he looked up at the preacher and smiled. "Thank you, my dear friend, for helping me discover my faith."

In this story the very religious belief and activity that the businessman engaged in is precisely what enabled him to avoid directly confronting his public engagement with the world. It is only in the removal of the seeming site of resistance that he was able to face his actions without supplement and reject them, helping him in turn to find a new way of living. In this parable we see the enactment of a Hegelian dialectic in which God (the affirmation) is negated in favor of humanism, a move that is itself negated at the end. The result of this negation of negation is that one's denial of God's place becomes the means of affirming God as dwelling in every place. Through a simple shift in perspective, God's nonpresence is affirmed as God's omnipresence and the sacred/secular divide is overcome. It is in this manner that we should affirm the insight of Karl Marx when he writes,

Criticism has plucked the imaginary flowers from the chain not so that man will wear the chain without any fantasy or consolation but so that he will shake off the chain and cull the living flower. The criticism of religion disillusions man to make him think and act and shape his reality like a man who has been disillusioned and has come to reason, so that he will revolve round himself and therefore round his true sun. . . . The task of history, therefore, once the world beyond the truth has disappeared, is to establish the truth of this world. The immediate task of philosophy, which is at the service of history, once the saintly form of human self-alienation has been unmasked, is to unmask self-alienation in its unholy forms. Thus the critique of heaven turns into the critique of earth.[3]

Here Marx understands that religious activity itself helps us to accept and work within an oppressive system and that the first step to breaking free from the oppression is to remove the flowers and accept the situation for what it is. This is also why Nietzsche calls alcohol and Christianity the "two great European narcotics," for both religious activities (as compartmentalized activities) and alcohol help us accept the situation we find ourselves in and thus dull the truly revolutionary act, the revolutionary act being that which does not work within the presently existing social structure but which places that social structure into question.

Moving beyond Conversation

So what has all this talk of irony and perverse transgression to do with emerging collectives? In my other chapter I explored some ideas that I see as central to some of the more radical emerging projects, projects that are interested not merely in manifesting some contemporary cultural version of evangelical thought but rather in moving beyond the limitations of contemporary evangelicalism and expressing a truly engaged "religionless" Christianity. The problem, however, is that such thinking is precisely that, thinking. The theoretical ideas are powerful; however, the ideas themselves do not help us avoid the ironic stance. Christianity promises not intellectual satisfaction but rather substantive transformation, that is, a qualitative change in our being that reconfigures our way of being in the world.

In order to move beyond the theoretical, various emerging collectives have been experimenting with what I call *transformance art*.

Transformance art can be described as an immersive art form that invites people to engage in a theatrical, ritualistic performance whereby they enact the death of God (as deus ex machina) and the resurrection of God (as one who dwells among us) with the purpose of reconfiguring one's social existence. Transformance art represents the attempt to subvert the ironic stance, providing a space for those who truly wish to enact a religionless Christianity rather than merely intellectually affirm it. It attempts to symbolically enact the negation of negation at work in the later Bonhoeffer as a means of encouraging the reconfiguration of one's social existence. Or, more precisely, one can say that transformance art is a multisensory theatrical provocation designed to cut against the gap between belief and action, offering substantive transformation. It aims to express and symbolically enact the logic of incarnation, in which the word is made manifest in fleshly activity.

Transformance art does not aim to change what we consciously think but rather to change the context that informs our action. In order to understand this, let us turn to an insightful anecdote that Žižek is fond of telling.

> There was once a man who met with a psychotherapist once a week for years because he was convinced that he was a seed. Eventually, after many years, he became convinced that he was really a human being. After thanking the therapist, he returned home happy. However, two weeks later the therapist heard a loud banging on the door. When he opened it, he saw the man back again, sweating and breathing heavily.
>
> "You have to help me," said the man. "My next-door neighbors recently bought chickens, and I am terrified that they are going to eat me."
>
> "But surely you know now that you are a human being and not seed," replied the therapist.
>
> "I know that," he replied. "But do the chickens know?"

This anecdote helps to draw out the way that we can intellectually disavow our beliefs while continuing to affirm them in our actions. Take the example of fashion. Most of us would agree that keeping up with the latest fashion can be a hollow and expensive pursuit. The problem is that as soon as we walk away from a conversation about it, we continue to act as if it were important and worthy of our time. The point then is not to convince ourselves of this fact but rather to convince the big other, who acts as the placeholder of this belief. In short, the point is to convince the magazines and advertisers of this fact. In a similar way, there are numerous churches in which the majority of people attending would broadly agree with the theology I outlined in my previous contribution to this volume. They would say that it is obvious we need to embrace doubt, live fully in the world, and abandon the sacred/secular divide. The problem is not to convince those within the church but rather to convince *the church itself*: the building, the ecclesial structure, the liturgies, and the creeds. The pews need to be convinced, the stained-glass windows, the pulpit, and the altar. Of course, chickens, magazines, and church buildings do not have beliefs, but they can act as the placeholders for our beliefs. And so by transforming them we can facilitate a transformation in our social selves.

Against this backdrop, we can begin to understand the role of transformance art. It is also against this background that we can understand why the emerging conversation has gradually begun taking on a different form, so much so that the phrase "emerging conversation" is rarely heard today and terms like "emerging cohorts" are becoming common. The reason for this can at least partially be ascribed to the fact that conversation and dialogue can only achieve so much. Indeed, such conversations can often end up being an impotent, anemic activity that increases our "understanding" without actually addressing concrete injustice.

From Emerging Conversation to Transformance Art

In light of this, various people associated with the emerging conversation have begun to develop what I refer to here as *transformance art*. While such groups create space for interesting discussions on such matters as theology, the environment, and political theory, and while they are often involved in social justice projects, the heart of these communities lies in their transformance art events.

Transformance art lies at the center of the communal experience of UK groups like ikon, The Garden, Grace, and Vaux, because here participants are challenged to live wholly in the world, to make sure that they do not merely engage in a weekly activity but rather bring liberation into every part of their lives. This does not negate activities such as voluntary work, but it demands that voluntary work emanate from a whole life dedicated to transforming an unjust system rather than simply being the way in which we abdicate our responsibility.

For those groups engaged in developing transformance art, the point is not to provide a space for people to engage in acts of love but rather to help reconfigure one's social existence so that acts of love become part of our whole existence.

Transformance art seeks to undermine the ironic stance in which one actively ridicules one's dominant social activity. It rejects any moves that would seek to remove us from the world. However, it also rejects a total immersion in the world. Instead, it encourages us to be fully immersed in the world in a manner that breaks open and reconfigures that world.

Convincing the Architecture

In many ways transformance art is simply a new name used to identify a practice that has existed for as long as civilization itself. Here I have in mind dramatic, ritualistic practices designed not to draw people *out of* the world but to invite transformative participation *in* the world. The practices I have in mind are designed to encourage and invite the incarnation of our ideals in our social existence. This is something that many parts of the established church already understand. Indeed, this can at least partially explain why emerging groups are growing up within many of the mainline churches (e.g., Anglo-emergents, Presbymergents).

People within emerging collectives are interested in both mystical theology and monastic life; however, this interest is grounded in material concerns, thus challenging the mystical-worldly divide. In the dialectic of emerging collectives, mystical practices are affirmed only inasmuch as they invite engagement with the world rather than turning from it.

One key ingredient to transformance art is physical location. Many emerging collectives take place in coffee shops, pubs, live-music venues, and a few even in art galleries. There are various reasons for this, some pragmatic. However, by changing the context within which church takes place, one changes how people interact as church. In many respects the majority of people in any reasonably reflective church community will advocate the idea that faith should be played out in the world rather than closeted away, that the body of Christ should be more welcoming and open to others, more embracing of difference, and more open to doubt, complexity, and ambiguity. Indeed, such values will often be heard emanating from the preacher on any given Sunday morning. Yet we all know that actually living these ideals out within a church building is difficult. The point is not then to simply change the people in the church building but rather to change the church building itself. We don't need to be convinced; *the architecture itself needs to be convinced.*

In a bar or café it is often easier for people to chat honestly about their lives. Many people feel more comfortable entering such spaces and are better able to talk about their doubts, pains, and uncertainties. Cafés and bars are the type of social space in which people have engaged in such conversations for years. The very act of meeting in such places has the effect of transforming how a gathering of people attempting to follow the way of Christ interact with one another and the wider community. One could set up a series of talks about how the church needs to be a place where people can sit together and chat about life, where they can invite friends without fear that they will feel alienated, or one can simply set up a group in a bar and witness how such things happen naturally.

By changing the context, one helps to facilitate a change in those who are meeting. What once seemed difficult, if not impossible, suddenly feels natural and easy. Instead of banging one's head against the wall by trying to get people to talk to one another, be open, express their hopes and fears, one can begin by changing the structure to one that emanates those values. Then what once seemed impossible slowly becomes not simply possible but inevitable.

In transformance art there is an intentional desire to form rituals and inhabit spaces that embody commitments to the world, to humility, doubt, and complexity. It is not brainwashing but body washing, helping us to become what we already believe.

So if emerging collectives are exploring the theology of worldly Christianity around tables late at night, then they are also beginning to develop and to rediscover innovative ways to help these ideas percolate into one's social existence. Criticisms of emerging collectives often focus on their tendency to emphasize talking over action; as these nascent experiments in transformance art begin to grow, however, hopefully such criticisms will ring less and less true.

Bible and Doctrine | Part 4

7

Scripture in the Emerging Movement

Scot McKnight

You could blame my interest in the emerging movement on Ginny Olson, my colleague who both invited me to a small group discussion with Brian McLaren on our campus and suggested that I begin reading up on the emerging movement. Then I had coffee with Bob Smietana, at that time an editor with the *Covenant Companion*, and he suggested that I begin "blogging," and I had to ask him what a "blog" was. But I blame my involvement on being a college professor with students who come by "emerging" Christianity naturally. But blogging, which I began in April 2005, led me into one layer after another of what the emerging movement was all about.

I began reading blogs to see what blogging was, and the blogs I read were those by "TSK" (Andrew Jones), Tony Jones, Steve McCoy, and others, and they led me in one way or another into discussions about the emerging movement. More importantly, they led me to discussions *by* emerging thinkers and leaders and pastors, and contact with such folks and blogs led me to say, "These are my kind of people." Though I don't think I began the practice, I began blogging through books by looking at one chapter per post and seeking to generate a conversation. The book that got my blog going on the emerging front was an advance copy of D. A. Carson's book *Becoming Conversant with the Emergent Church*. From that review onward, I have considered myself part of the emerging conversation.

What attracted me? The willingness to question things, even sacred things. The desire to get Christianity back on track with Jesus's vision for the kingdom. An embrace of a more humble epistemology, what Lesslie Newbigin called a "proper confidence." The recognition, even radical at times, of the importance and centrality of hermeneutics to all things Christian. A fearlessness about working out a Christian political vision. The unquestioned willingness to embrace a theology and a gospel that knows God's preferential option for the poor. And, finally, a radical commitment to a missional approach to the church.

When I began peering into the emerging movement, I was being asked by one and all what I thought would become of things emerging, and I said at that time what I think has more or less happened: first, some would simply walk into the mainline approach to American Christianity; others would walk away from the faith, and my book *Finding Faith, Losing Faith* (with Hauna Ondrey) examines that issue; and yet others would walk in such a manner that evangelical churches would embrace a nobler and more holistic gospel approach to ministry. I believe the emerging movement is here to stay, but it will continue to morph in new directions, not all of them in ways I'd prefer to see them morphing.

Introduction

Traditionally, pastors have been taught how to read the Bible through what we now call "exegesis," the careful analysis—word by word, sentence by sentence, paragraph by paragraph—of the Bible in its original languages and in its original settings. Pastors were trained so that they could become professionals, including professionals in their Bible reading. Traditionally, parishioners were taught to read the Bible daily and devotionally. The occasional pastor, riding on the crest of seminary excitement and convinced that he had figured out how to read the Bible well, urged his parishioners to learn Hebrew and Greek with the hope that they would become better Bible readers. Most such pastors calmed down to reality after one or two years, and they had to learn to put up with the oddities of lay Bible reading and even their own oddities. Those oddities need special attention because they help us read the Bible better. I'd like to sketch five such oddities of Bible reading, and I do so because how one reads the Bible shapes one's spirituality just as much as one's spirituality shapes how one reads the Bible.[1] These five oddities in Bible reading emerge from my own experience in teaching churches and students how to read the Bible.

How the Bible Is Read in the Church Today

For some people the Bible is *the lawbook*. This approach to Bible reading operates with the lessons learned on Sinai: God speaks; God's people are to do what God speaks. That there are *imperatives* in the Bible no one contests—think of Exodus 20 and Leviticus 19 and Deuteronomy 6, or pick a snippet or two from a prophet like Micah or Isaiah or Haggai, or read for just a few moments in the Sermon on the Mount or ponder Galatians 5–6 or begin counting commands in James. These imperatives are not just wisdom snippets for the church's consideration but are taken by traditional Christians as God commanding God's people. The issue is not the presence of imperatives but the *place imperatives play in one's perception of the Bible and how one proceeds through the Bible*. For some it is mostly about commands and prohibitions. Some read the Bible with this simple prayer to God: "Tell me what to do!" More often than not, law book readers of the Bible develop a spirituality in which God is the Lawgiver and Commander above all chiefs. Pastors who prefer a sense of authority about their role in the local church and community often buttress this form of Bible reading by the way they speak and carry out their tasks. Spirituality for such folks focuses on obedience and conformity; the nonconformist is apostate. There are words for this approach to the Christian life, and many of them are not good. Still, the Bible has commands; God does give laws; God's people are to listen and do. But there is more to the Bible than laws.

For others the Bible is a *collection of blessings and promises.* These folks, pastors and laypersons, open up their Bibles with this little prayer: "Tell me something nice!" What they are looking for they find. Stephanus, in 1551, divided the Bible into verses, and they find verses that tell them nice things—God blessing them and God promising them good things. There are many wonderful blessings in the Bible, and I think of the blessings of Deuteronomy 28 and the Beatitudes and great promises like the covenant formula, "I will be your God and you will be my people," caught up as it is in the drama of Hosea 1–2. Or the words of Jesus that he will be with his disciples until the end of all ends in Matthew 28:16–20. And we need these blessings and promises, daily and devotionally. But there is more to the Bible than blessings and promises. Reading the Bible with that aim in mind produces a God who is the Grand Dispenser of Good Things, a kind of Mr. Rogers in the Sky. Furthermore, this kind of Bible reading produces happiness in happy people but very little sympathy for those who struggle mightily with depression or death or divorce or disappointments. Ironically, the two most famous collections of blessings in the Bible, the Mosaic blessings of Deuteronomy 28 and Jesus's Beatitudes, are connected to curses as well. As there are wonderful stories, so there are stories like Job and exile and persecution and the cross itself. Reading the Bible just for blessings and promises distorts what the Bible itself is. Calendar companies may provide us with a blessing a day, but Jeremiah's calendar may have offered a warning of God's wrath each day.

Yet another tendency is to see the Bible itself as a *Rorschach ink-blot.* Hermann Rorschach (1884–1922), a Swiss Freudian psychiatrist, designed a series of inkblots to show his clients. They were really only blobs of ink pressed against a blank sheet to form a perfect symmetry. He asked his clients to tell him what they saw, and since the inkblots really were nothing, whatever the client saw came from his or her mind, heart, and soul. Presto! Revelations could occur, problems diagnosed, and remedies designed. Presto! is really Projection! Which leads me to an observation about how some folks read the Bible: they project onto the Bible what is really inside their minds, hearts, and souls. What they see is what they want instead of what is there. For such folks, one simple prayer (and here we are dipping into Freud's approach by searching for unconscious clues) will do: "Tell me I'm OK!" They read the Bible to confirm what they think and to affirm who they are. A standardized exam I give to my Jesus of Nazareth students is a simple psychology exam with a twist: the second half of the exam asks the student to answer the same questions for Jesus. The wonder of this exam is that there are no "right" answers, but it illuminates what we think is the "right" answer: namely, that most people think Jesus is like themselves because most have the same answers for Jesus as they had for themselves.[2] In other words, Presto! Bible reading is Projection! For such persons God is the Great Affirmer, and spirituality is about self-affirmation through self-discovery. I exaggerate, of course, but the general direction of this form of Bible reading lends itself to a spirituality focused on self-affirmation.

I move now to two more-sophisticated forms of Bible reading, the first of which is reading the Bible as a *massive puzzle*. Thomas Jefferson famously cut up his Bible into acceptable and unacceptable verses. Biblical puzzlers just cut the Bible up into verses, spread them out (metaphorically speaking) on a huge gym floor, and then begin to gather them into the System Behind the Bible that explains the Bible better than the Bible itself. The one who explains the most verses wins. Instead of reading the Bible as the unfolding, uneven, contoured story of God's redemption in this world, these folks belong to the Flat Bible Society and think that the primary reason God gave the Bible was to reveal a system of truth. Once that System is discerned the whole Bible makes sense—except the parts that don't fit into the System, and they are always left out. I am, now that the cat is out of the bag, criticizing the way *some* (not all) do systematic theology. Had God wanted us to read the Bible as the Grand System, I suspect God would have given us a Systematic Theology. He did not, and I suspect we need to learn to read the Bible *as God gave it—as a collection of books from Genesis to Revelation*.[3] The folks who treat the Bible as a puzzle to be solved, glued, and then framed have this prayer: "Teach me the System!" A distinct form of spirituality, not all bad, emerges from this form of Bible reading: an intellectual, heady theory of the Christian life that genuinely believes if we have the right ideas, we will live more godly lives. That is, such a spirituality is a form of cognitive behaviorism. God for them tends to be the Great Mind behind the Bible, a kind of Wizard of Oz.

Finally, others read the Bible *through their maestro.* I like to cook, and I consider myself an amateur specialist in making risotto, an Italian way of preparing rice. My wife, Kris, and I recently spent a week in Italy on vacation, and I ate risotto every evening, sampling the recipe of each restaurant's cook's way of making risotto. My intent was to see how a *maestro di cucina*, a master of the art of Italian cooking, makes risotto so I could improve my own risotto. In Stresa, near Lago Maggiore on the northern tip of Italy, we went to Ristorante Fiorentino. Carla Bolongaro welcomed us and seated us and served us while her son, Luigino, the *maestro di cucina*, prepared our dinner. All risottos are prepared in thick-bottomed pans; the starches of the rice are drawn out from the Carnaroli or Arborio rice with broth one ladle at a time. Luigino added saffron and some tasty prosciutto along with some bits of porcini mushroom, and by the time we left we knew we had tasted risotto at its finest. I don't tell you this to make you hungry, nor to tell you that I have several times done my best to imitate the risotto recipe of the Bolongaro family, but to say that many read the Bible the way they learn from a *maestro di cucina.* That is, they go to the Bible to find the master, the über-rabbi—Jesus—at work and when they get up from their reading of the Bible, they imitate Maestro Jesus. "What would Jesus do?" is the only question they ask. (The problem here is the word *only.*)

It is almost justifiable to make Jesus the maestro. But more than a few of us are aware that Jesus has been eclipsed for many Bible readers (read: Reformed) by Maestro Paul. In this way of reading the Bible, Jesus is either ignored or overwhelmed by Paul's way of thinking. Some of us grew up in churches where the thought patterns, the lenses, the grid through which everything was filtered—however unconsciously—was the book of Romans or Paul's theology (as understood, of course, by Calvin or Luther). I am one such person because I grew up in a Pauline church (except when it came to drinking wine). Even when we dipped into the Gospels, especially at Christmas and Easter, we used Maestro Paul to inform us about what Jesus was really doing and saying. I cannot tell you what it was like when, as a first-year seminary student, I sat under Walt Liefeld and listened—at

7:45 a.m., with my jaw agape—to someone who could open up the world of Jesus for me. Right then and there, in the deepest recesses of my own soul, I knew I had found my life's passion: to study and teach about Jesus. I had been tutored under Maestro Paul, and I found Jesus, who (I now admit) became another Maestro. Reading the Bible through a maestro's eyes gives us one chapter in the story of the Bible. One-chapter Bible readers develop one-chapter Christian lives. God becomes the God of Jesus or the God of Paul—not the multivarianted God of Moses *and* David *and* Isaiah *and* Jesus *and* Paul *and* Hebrews *and* John *and* James. Spirituality becomes shaped narrowly by one set of categories, say Paul's soteriological thinking (like Lutherans and the Reformed and evangelicals) or Jesus's kingdom thinking (like Anabaptists and liberals) or James's Torah-shaped thinking (like messianic Jews) . . . and I could go on. The point is that maestro reading of the Bible is narrow and less than the ideal. The prayer before Bible reading here is "Give me a theologian I can trust!"

An Emerging Concern in Bible Reading: The Linguistic Turn

Now that I have criticized these various oddities in Bible reading I am forced to say how I think we *ought* to read the Bible. Before I do that, I want to insert into this discussion that we are concerned with how people in the emerging movement read the Bible, and I get to beg off by saying there is no such thing as "an emerging reading of the Bible." Which is customary rhetoric for those of us who think the emerging, or postevangelical, movement shows promise not only for deconstruction but also for some positive reconstruction at the level of church praxis and theology. So what I offer is *one emerging way of Bible reading,* and I want to draw on one major theme of the emerging movement, namely, postmodernity's linguistic turn.[4] That is, it is all about hermeneutics and how language works and how language itself is both adequate and yet always limited.

To get this point across, I appeal to one of America's finest Bible scholars, the Jewish professor at the University of Chicago Michael Fishbane and his newest book *Sacred Attunement.*[5] After saying that the word *tree* is not the tree itself but only a "hint or pointer toward

it," that is, "only a conventional sound signifying this tangible reality,"
Fishbane proceeds to God-talk: "If this is true of ordinary speech,
whose focus is the common world and ordinary frames of reference,
how much more is it true of theological speech, which attempts to
designate God with names and epithets?" This is a question that
emerging folks want to ask and will not let go; they know it has an
impact on how we read the Bible, and they also suspect—because of
raised eyebrows and some false accusations about relativity—that
this linguistic turn really does make a difference. Fishbane goes on:

> Humans have at hand a bundle of everyday words and terms. But which
> one would turn the trick and name God and divine activity? If all the
> world were ink and all our speech quills,[6] and if we were ever able to
> denote all that we and the entirety of humankind has ever thought and
> felt about divine reality, could we ever truly express or indicate God?
> And if all the world were sound and all our words could articulate the
> totality of these sounds, in some majestic polyphonic concordance,
> could we ever articulate or intone God?

Fishbane then moves to his conclusion about both the adequacy of
language and its limitations: "The arcs of speech are thus always
curving toward the mystery of expression and the gap between words
and their references—and all the more so as one tries to express the
ineffable reality of God in human language." I adore his closing line,
expressing as it does an almost Eastern Orthodox sense of apophatic
theology and theologizing: "As the curve of speech bends toward the
transcendent, this truth [about God] becomes ever more unsayable."
   Fishbane helpfully connects this hermeneutical spirituality to prayer
with these words: "In such a way, the process of prayer keeps one alert
to the fragility of speech and its necessities in all areas of life; but it
can also simultaneously help one remember the role of language as
signs between our eyes of the sacred mysteries of existence, which
we call to mind through names and terms and epithets." Such an approach to Bible reading and prayer calls for epistemic humility. Again,
Fishbane: "All of which suggests that while the world is there for our
discernment, and does not resist our inferences, one should respond
to it with great theological humility." To recall his own a fortiori,
or *qal vahomer*, point: if this is the case with our discerning use of

language for the world, how much more so with the Bible and God! In fact, Fishbane's own hermeneutic, grounded as it is in a profound sense of how language works, leads all "exegesis" and "theology" and "prayer" and "Bible reading" to its proper end: silence. Here now his words, or to use the language of the synagogue: *Ta shema*, come and hear!

> We live within the darkness of unknowing.
> "Bless the Lord, O my soul" is the final word. It is the aim of the religious spirit and the goal of covenant theology.
> [This] is the silence of the white spaces between words or vocables of scripture; it is the silence of Job who realized that he "spoke without knowledge"; and it is also the silence of the psalmist who said, "To you silence [*dummiyah*] is praise" (Ps. 65:2). All this is utter silence. It is a radical spiritual caesura, without echo or earthly sound. It pervades consciousness, and is not the prelude to speech in any sense.

So what is the call of the Bible reader who knows the finitude of language, who knows that the cheap tricks of the shortcuts I mentioned above simply do not come to the proper end of genuine encounter with the thrice-mysterious God we worship? Fishbane points the way, and with this I'll be done with his book:

> The challenge here is to endure the terror of concealment. This is not a silence of why or wherefore; it is simply silence. Nor is it a silence of waiting or expectation; it is simply being silent within the concealment, in the uttermost spiritual stillness.
> This is *shetiqah*: an absolute stillness and speechlessness within the Void, beyond words. But it is also an ascendant silence, rising toward God's Absolute Transcendence. Caesura is its name.

I must admit that my own take on these things is not as profound as Fishbane's. Like the Delphic oracle, Fishbane knows whereof he speaks, and I think I've tasted his caesura, the chasm between what we say about God and what we come up against as we come to its proper end in worship. Because I have seen this cliff, I know the five images I gave above are simply not enough. What each assumes is an almost absolute adequacy not only of a specific set of terms but of the reader's (sometimes cocky) comprehension and understanding of those terms. Whether one wants to call it the linguistic turn and anchor it in postmodernity or not is hardly my concern here. Eastern Orthodoxy's apophaticism, Fishbane's Jewish reverence for words as tools that lead us to God, and the emerging movement's commitments justify the critique of the earlier mentioned ways of reading the Bible. Yet from both the Orthodox and Fishbane I have a word of warning to the emerging crowd: commitment to the linguistic turn and its profound impact on hermeneutics and Bible reading *dare not lead to arrogance.* It leads one to drink from a well that cannot be drained, to an ocean that is too vast for words, and to a God who is so distant and holy and unapproachable that reverence is the only proper entailment of an emerging understanding of Scripture. It leads to epistemic humility, another set of words for reverence of the mind. Sadly, reverence is not what the emerging movement is known for. Instead, its only partial, youthful grip on the linguistic turn has led too many to an informal, insolent, supercilious affectation. Giving youth the linguistic turn can be like giving teenagers sex—until the mysteries of love are experienced, the linguistic turn sours. To carry this further: the linguistic turn is an intoxicant; you either know your limits and respect them, or you fall into a drunken stupor from which you may never recover.

With this interlude on the linguistic turn and its influence on the emerging movement's understanding of Bible reading, I turn now to an idea that may help us bring Bible reading and the emerging movement to a point of consensus.

Wiki-Stories of the Story

I said I was done with Fishbane, but that was only that section of *Sacred Attunement.* Jewish rabbis and scholars make a distinction between written Torah, oral Torah, and the Torah of all-in-all.[7] That is, between *torah she-bikhtav, torah she-be'al peh,* and *torah kelulah,* that is, between God's written Word, the divinely guided *interpretation* of God's Word, and *the limitation of both written Word and interpreted Word for articulating the utter infinitude of God's truth.*

It strikes me that this Jewish theology of Scripture and God's communication with us in this world fits into an emerging understanding of reading the Bible. How so? We have the text, the Bible itself; we have "our plot" that ties the Bible together so that we can comprehend the text; and we have the Story that God is telling, which the Scripture itself also tells but never completely. I rely here on the words of the apostle Paul: he tells us that God's revelation is a gracious "mystery" that was only made known with clarity in Christ (Eph. 3:3). That is, the age of Torah was only a partial disclosure of God's mysterious plan in Christ. And even here there is inadequacy or limitation, and I quote from Ephesians 3:18–19: "I pray that you may have the power to comprehend, with all the saints, what is the breadth and length and height and depth, and to know the love of Christ that surpasses knowledge, so that you may be filled with all the fullness of God." This mystery, wrought with inadequate language, leads to worship: "Now to him who by the power at work within us is able to accomplish abundantly far more than all we can ask or imagine, to him be glory in the church and in Christ Jesus to all generations, forever and ever. Amen" (vv. 20–21). Paul knows that his knowledge is only partial, as 1 Corinthians 13:12 makes abundantly clear: "For now we see in a mirror, dimly, but then we will see face to face. Now I know only in part; then I will know fully, even as I have been fully known." Theology and Bible reading are part of a "mirror, dimly, but then" kind of knowledge. Admission of this is not a denial of the truth of the Bible but a confession of epistemic humility even of the Bible's witness to the truth of the gospel.

I trade now in Fishbane's a fortiori: if Paul can say that his own grasp of the gospel is "dim," then we must conclude that the Bible itself is a dim witness to the ultimate (presently) unsayable truth of God. And if this is the case with written Scripture, it is also the case with our interpretation of Scripture. Both Scripture and interpretation are "dim" articulations of a truth that will surpass what we now know. This doesn't make our gospel truth wrong; it makes our gospel truth only a partial grasp of the ultimate truth.

Now I suggest that we replace Fishbane's *Torah* with the word *Story* and ponder an emerging understanding of Bible reading and Scripture hermeneutics. In brief, it goes like this:

The ultimate truth is "the Story."

The written truth is made up of "wiki-stories."

The oral truth, our interpretation of the wiki-stories, our plots of the wiki-stories, is "church tradition."

Now a confession of how I learned to read the Bible as wiki-stories. For many years, instead of grasping the Bible as Story, I was a maestro Bible reader. I learned to tame the other authors of the Bible by making them all sound like Maestro Jesus, the über-rabbi. At times I sneaked into the cabins of others for a meal or two with other cooks; that is, I wrote commentaries on Galatians and 1 Peter. During this time I nursed a secret (and never expressed) grudge against two authors who, for me, were problems: the apostle Paul and the apostle John. Why? I believed they had *ignored* the kingdom message of Jesus. I was upset with them for using words like "justification" and "church" and "eternal life"—not that there is anything wrong with these terms. So devoted was I to Maestro Jesus's verbal vision that I thought these other New Testament writers should have used Jesus's pet expression, namely, "kingdom of God." I could not understand why Paul dropped words like "disciple" or why he seemed to ignore the Sermon on the Mount or why John translated "kingdom" into "eternal life." So I tamed them by using only Jesus's words.

Furthermore, as a maestro reader of the Bible I also nursed a grudge against the puzzlers of this world, and my grudge emerged from two convictions about how to read the Bible. First (and I still sense this at times), those who have a solved puzzle rarely let Jesus's kingdom message be what it was. To say this another way: kingdom language does not unfold as easily into systematic categories. My second problem was that every approach I have read by puzzlers somehow managed to avoid the story and the plot as the central categories for knowing the message of the Bible. Instead of creation and fall, exodus and exile, community and redemption, the Story was flattened out. Categories like God, man, Christ, sin, salvation, and eschatology were pieced together from various authors and, in my view, the authors themselves were not given their day before the jury. I congratulated myself for being hyperbiblical about Jesus's message of the kingdom, which I thought was better than the puzzling approach, but while I was fair to Jesus, I didn't have an approach that let each author in the Bible tell his own story.

But that all changed when I discovered the linguistic turn's significance, that is, when I realized that God chose to communicate with us *in language*. This may seem either profoundly obvious, on the level of the person who says the sky is above us, or profoundly profound. It was "profoundly profound" for me. And this is why it changed how I read the Bible: since God chose to communicate in language, and since language is always shaped by context, and since God chose to speak to us over time through many writers, then God also chose to speak to us in a variety of ways and expressions. Furthermore, I believe that because the gospel Story is so deep and wide, *God needed a variety of expressions to give us a fuller picture of the Story.*

This liberated me from the maestro approach and drove me to the wiki-story approach of reading the Bible. I now know that the various versions of the Story in the Bible need to be seen for what they are: wiki-stories of the Story. In our Bible, God did what God has always done: he spoke in Moses's days in Moses's ways, in Micah's days in Micah's ways, and in Jesus's days in Jesus's ways. Which meant that when Paul came around, Paul got to speak in Paul's ways for Paul's days, and when John put quill to parchment, he was freed up to speak in John's ways for John's days. This discovery liberated me and (to use some puns) it justified Paul and gave new life to John to take Jesus's kingdom story and make it their own story of the Story. I've come to see these stories of the Story to be like the seventh day of creation, very, very good. No single story, not even Jesus's, can tell the whole Story. We need them all.

So, you ask, why see the various authors as wiki-stories? Most of us are familiar with Wikipedia. Wikipedia has its detractors and its problems, but that won't keep the world or our students (or any of us) from using it. It is a collaborative, democratic, interactive, developing encyclopedia to which anyone in the world, ostensibly, can make a contribution. It is not like your father's encyclopedia, whether that was the *World Book* or *Encyclopedia Britannica*. Instead, an entry in Wikipedia can change daily: paragraphs can be deleted and entries can be completely rewritten or new entries added. It is sometimes called "open source." Because it is truly "open," bad information can filter into the entries and render their quality suspect. In calling the Bible a wiki-story, I will bracket off the problems of bad contributors to Wikipedia.

All I want to focus on here is one element: the *ongoing reworking of the biblical Story by new authors so that they can speak the old story in new ways for their days. I contend the Bible is like this: it is an ongoing series of retellings of the One True Story that never has a final, unrevisable shape.*

If you would like a more Jewish way of saying each author is a writer of a wiki-story, I would say the Bible contains an ongoing series of *midrashes*, or interpretive retellings, of the one Story God wants us to know and hear. Each biblical author, whether we talk of Moses and the Pentateuch, or the so-called Deuteronomic Histories, or the Chronicler, Job or Ecclesiastes, or the various prophets, or Jesus or Paul or John or James or the author of Hebrews or Peter . . . each of these authors tells his version of the Story. They tell wiki-stories of the Story; they give midrashes on the previous stories. Sometimes one author picks up the story of someone else, as when the Chronicler picks up 1–2 Kings and recasts it. Or when Isaiah picks up Micah and Hosea. But other times we have more or less a new story, as with Daniel or Jeremiah or Ezekiel or the apostle Paul or the writer of Hebrews.

To reemphasize: there is no one final wiki-story that becomes the Story to which all the others, like the brothers to Joseph, must submit. All we have are wiki-versions of the One True Story.

If you would like to see this in action, open your Bible to Matthew 4:1–11, Matthew's version of the temptations of Jesus. What Matthew does here is tell a wiki-story, a new version, of an old story. Many—far too many in fact—have been taught this passage in a blessings/promises or Rorschach approach. They have been taught to read this text for themselves and for their own personal enrichment—as a method for responding to temptations to sin. They have learned this: the biblical answer to facing temptation, which is never even remotely mentioned in the text itself, is to quote the Bible at Satan when we are tempted. This makes sense, but it has nothing to do with the text itself. Instead, whether applicable directly to life or not—which by the way entirely dominates how many read the Bible—the singular question the Story asks us is one of two options: Is Jesus's temptation the reliving of Adam and Eve's experience in Eden? (Jesus is then cast as the second Adam, only perfectly obedient, and thereby the pioneer of a new Adamic line.) Or, which is more probable, is Jesus's temptation the reliving of Israel's wilderness testings? (Jesus is then recast as the second Israel, leading his people to a new promised land.) Thus, in either case, Matthew casts Jesus as an updated version, a wiki-story, of an older story, either the Eden story or the wilderness story. To read the Bible this way is to learn to read each text as part of a lengthy set of texts, to read each text as an element in a wiki-story that is encompassed by both other wiki-stories and the Story itself.

Many New Testament specialists will tell you that nearly every page of the New Testament is a wiki-story on an Old Testament wiki-story. In fact, the Old Testament scholar John Goldingay says the New Testament is nothing but footnotes on the Old Testament![8] He adds that "one cannot produce a theology out of footnotes." That is, if you do not have the Old Testament in your head, you cannot grasp what the New Testament authors are saying. (Goldingay, as is typical with him, exaggerates to make a point—only he might not say he's exaggerating.)

Here's where we are:

The Bible is a Story.

The Story is made up of a series of wiki-stories.

The wiki-stories are held together by the Story.

We comprehend the wiki-stories and the Story by framing a plot that holds the wiki-stories together. (A plot is not the same as a system.)

Now here is a decidedly emerging conclusion: none of the wiki-stories is final; none of them is comprehensive; none of them is absolute; none of them is exhaustive. The maestro approach tries to make them so; so also the puzzle approach. But these approaches fail: the first for making one author the dominant author; the second for making *our version of the Story* the final version. Each author in the Bible tells *a true story of that Story*, but none of them gets to tell the final wiki-story to end all wiki-stories. And that is why we need to read the Bible, not by puzzling it out or by finding a maestro, but by summoning each author of the Bible to the table to let each tell his version of the Story.

My contention, of course, is that this partakes in the linguistic turn. Namely, one reason we must read the Bible as wiki-stories is because no one set of terms can tell the whole Story completely. We need different stories to get the Story across. Sure, there is a plot, but that plot is our plotting of the wiki-stories instead of any one author's plot. Most of us would agree that the general plot looks like this:

- First, God created us as Eikons (image of God), and we were at one with God, self, others, and the world.

- Second, Adam and Eve cracked the Eikon by choosing to sin against God, and this led to alienation from God, self, others, and the world. Oneness is broken through sin.

- Third, God chose to restore cracked Eikons with himself, with themselves, with others, and with the world *by forming a covenant community*, called Israel and kingdom and church in the Bible. This restoration is designed for oneness.

- Fourth, God restores cracked Eikons (again, with himself, themselves, others, and the world) through the life, death, and resurrection of Jesus Christ and through the mighty empowerment of the Spirit—and Jesus is the perfect Eikon (2 Cor. 3:18–4:4; Col. 1:15–17). Oneness, in other words, is only formed in being "one in Christ" (Gal. 3:18).

- Fifth, and finally, God's restoring process is only completed at the consummation when we fully love God and fully love ourselves and fully love others and dwell in the world as God designed for us. Then we will be at one with God, with self, with others, and with the world.

This plot, I suggest, is adequate to hold all the wiki-stories together, but it is also my plot and my way of putting this together, and I am quite happy to say that many—the church tradition aspect of reading the Bible—read the Bible this way. In fact, I was taught to read the Bible this way—more or less. But we dare not equate the wiki-stories with our plot. So there is both a claim to adequacy here and a further claim to inadequacy, namely, a recognition that our plot is our plot and not God's plot. Our plotting of the wiki-stories, to be sure, curves upward toward the Story itself insofar as it respects and restates those wiki-stories in faithful ways, but it remains our plot.

The Story itself, God's Story of truth, transcends the wiki-stories and surely transcends our plotting of those wiki-stories. Each wiki-story tells a true story of the Story so that it is adequate, but no one wiki-story tells the Story in final form. We can speak with boldness because the wiki-stories are true and adequate; we are to speak with humility because our plotting of the wiki-stories remains *ours and not God's*.

Here is where worship joins us. Our task as Bible readers is to be like Ruth. Elimelech married Naomi, and they had two boys, Mahlon and Chilion. Times were tough, so they left Bethlehem and moved to Moab, where both boys found wives, one named Orpah (Oprah Winfrey's mom spelled her name wrong) and one named Ruth. The men finked out on the women and died—all three of them. Naomi gathered her daughters-in-law together and said, "Go back home and I'll move back to Bethlehem to my people and we'll call it a chapter in life." Orpah took her advice and disappeared. Ruth hung on with these words, words that teach us how to read the Bible:

> Do not press me to leave you
> > or to turn back from following you!
> Where you go, I will go;
> > Where you lodge, I will lodge;
> your people shall be my people,
> > and your God my God.
>
> Where you die, I will die—
> > there will I be buried.
> May the LORD do thus and so to me,
> > and more as well,
> if even death parts me from you! (Ruth 1:16–17)

Ruth surrendered her life to the story of Naomi's people. She let Naomi's wiki-story be her wiki-story. Our task as Bible readers is to let the Bible's wiki-stories be ours so that our story becomes theirs and theirs becomes ours.

To worship is to enter into the Story by surrendering to the wiki-stories, both as biblical texts and as their faithful representations in our plottings. We listen to Moses and to David and to Micah and to Hosea and to Jesus and to Paul and to Peter, and we can scarce take it all in. But we listen, as we are called to do. In listening we are transformed, as the Story takes hold in our hearts through the various versions of the wiki-stories. We tell the stories by entering into the stories, and somehow, through the work of God's Spirit, the Story itself is told and revealed. Because there are so many wiki-stories and because we have no means of putting them all together into final form, we come to the end of our ropes, we settle into silence, and we hear, as from a distant mountain, clear echoes of the true Story, which redeems. In listening to those sounds, we find ourselves worshiping God and grateful for his Story and satisfied with the versions we have until that day.

8

Atonement and Gospel

Scot McKnight

I visited a church website recently and read the "what we believe" statements. What jumped off the page for me were the problems the statements created. The most emphatic assertion was the belief that Jesus is the Savior. From this the statements inferred that discipleship and the kingly reign of Christ and the church had nothing to do with salvation. Second, much of the remaining space was consumed with problems the statements had now created: yes, you must be obedient; no, it's not about your salvation; yes, you are called to be a disciple; no, it's not about your salvation; yes, Jesus is Lord; no, he doesn't have to be Lord to be Savior. The statements twisted every which way but simply couldn't come out and say, "If you don't follow Jesus, you can't enter into the kingdom." Yet as I read the statements, I was convinced that's exactly what the church believed, but it was afraid that acknowledging it would deny that salvation is totally by "grace" and totally by "faith." The church was struggling for a rhetoric that would put teeth into discipleship.

Running through it all were two themes: gospel and atonement (theory). That is, the gospel is rooted in an atonement theory, in this case penal substitution. How so? The gospel is that Jesus came to earth to die for our sins by absorbing God's wrath (penal substitution) and to make us right (justification via double imputation) with God. This was the "gospel" according to this church's statements.

As is the case with many evangelicals today, atonement theory and gospel are so interlocked one cannot separate them. Yet there are some serious debates today, like the new perspective on Paul, about this interlocking relationship, and these challenges are calling for a closer look at both gospel and atonement.

Various groups are debating their own concerns, but the emerging movement in the church is debating—though not always explicitly—the meaning of gospel. It goes like this: Jesus preached the gospel *of the kingdom*, but it appears that Paul preached the gospel *of salvation and justification by faith*. How do we connect the two? If the connection is difficult to sustain, and if the emerging movement is asked which to choose, my guess is that the vast majority of emerging Christians would choose Jesus and his vision of the kingdom, justice, peace, and love. Many, in fact, are doing just that—not so much in writing as with their feet and hands and actions. Involved in that choice is serious discussion about *how* atonement takes place, for I have heard time and time again from emerging friends that a God who must punish (out of holiness or justice) in order to forgive is morally objectionable. So for emerging Christians gospel and atonement are connected, and some wonder if atonement is even needed.

By the term *emerging* I don't want to limit myself to the rock stars—Brian McLaren, to name one—of the emerging church movement. I find this debate about gospel and atonement pervading various circles of the emerging movement, not the least of which is the "missional" movement. In a recent book edited (and created) by J. R. Woodward, *ViralHope: Good News from the Urbs to the Burbs (and Everything in Between)*, for which I wrote a foreword, there was a concentrated discussion of "gospel."[1] What struck me over and over as I read through the essays was how seldom *cross*, *atonement*, and especially *an atonement theory* seemed to be involved in the framing and discussion of the meaning of the word *gospel*. And I would classify the writers of these essays to be of a moderate group theologically, and at least among these writers, there is a struggle about the relationship of gospel and atonement. The more radical emerging types do not abandon atonement or atonement theory but rather reshape atonement theory into categories drawn from scholars like J. Moltmann, R. Girard, and J. Denny Weaver. To call this exploration "liberalism," as many critics of the emerging movement do, is to miss the point. What is at work most often is a more robust commitment to kingdom vision and an attempt to frame atonement within that larger commitment. I see it as an ongoing theological struggle but with no clearly defined position. Obviously, the emerging movement is seeking to connect gospel and atonement.

Another major issue today in the wider church debate about gospel and atonement is the famous term that rose to the top during the Reformation, *justification*. Often enough—if you listen carefully—the Reformed concern about the new perspective's broadening and depersonalizing of justification involves this interlocking relationship of gospel and atonement. At work in the (conservative and Reformed) evangelical gospel, then, are three terms examined in this chapter: *justification*, *propitiation*, and *gospel*. In one way or another, the first two are defining the third. I want to begin with this evangelical context before I move into my own studies on the relationship of gospel and atonement, which I hope will be given consideration in the emerging movement.

Justification and Propitiation

The theme of the 2003 Wheaton Theology Conference was "The Gospel, Freedom and Righteousness: The Doctrine of Justification."[2] The conference used all the right words and had all the right speakers; the first paper was by Robert Gundry, a veteran New Testament scholar known for his patient analysis of biblical evidence and courage to say what the Bible says and not be afraid if the Bible doesn't say enough. I was at work on an academic book about how Jesus understood his death,[3] and I had been drawn through that research into two issues that have shaped my own research and writing interests for nearly a decade: the meaning of *gospel* and *atonement theories*.

What Gundry had to say mattered to me because I knew his careful scholarship. He argued that double imputation is not supported in the New Testament. Rather, the New Testament texts teach that our sin is imputed to Christ but that Christ's righteousness is not imputed to us.

Second Corinthians 5:19 and 21 clinch the conclusion that our sins are imputed to Christ: "In Christ God was reconciling the world to himself, not counting their trespasses against them, and entrusting the message of reconciliation to us. . . . For our sake *he made him to be sin who knew no sin*, so that in him we might become the righteousness of God."

It seems logical, and all the Reformers were at one on this matter, that God imputed the sin of sinners to Christ in order to carry them away and forgive our sins. So far so good, and very Reformed and evangelical. But Gundry, against the grain, demonstrates that the New Testament evidence says our "faith" is "imputed" to us as righteousness and not Christ's righteousness, and one text illustrates the point he made that day: "Faith was reckoned to Abraham as righteousness" (Rom. 4:9).

Reformed thinking tends to argue that "faith" here is shorthand for faith being the human trigger for God's shifting of Christ's righteousness to our side of the ledger. Justification, then, is both positive and negative for Gundry: "Negatively, God does not count our sins against us. Jesus took them away. Positively, God counts our faith as righteousness."[4]

When Gundry sat down, D. A. Carson stood up to vindicate double imputation. Carson began with these words: "For many Protestants today, the doctrine of imputation [i.e., double] has become the crucial touchstone for orthodoxy with respect to justification."[5] Carson's admission is noteworthy. It comes by way of an almost deconstructive question addressed to Gundry by the time Carson wrapped up his presentation: "So why should a scholar who accepts that Paul teaches that our sins are imputed to Christ, even though no text explicitly says so, find it so strange that many Christians have held that Paul teaches that Christ's righteousness is imputed to us, even though no text explicitly says so?"[6]

I must confess that I side with Carson on this one. Paul, even if ambiguously, says in 1 Corinthians 1:30 that Christ is our righteousness, and he says in 2 Corinthians 5:21 that Christ was made sin on our behalf. These texts appear to me to reveal how it is that justification—a ledger metaphor—occurs. But what we should note here is one word: *ambiguous*. Or, put negatively, there is no unambiguous statement that his righteousness is imputed to us and nothing explicitly using *imputed* to say that our sins were shuffled onto his side of the ledger. Yet for many the heart of the gospel, yea the orthodox view of justification and the gospel itself, is at stake in this one.

So also for many with the word *propitiation*. Hear now the words of J. I. Packer, the dean of atonement theology among evangelicals (in the Reformed branch): "So how did the cross actually reconcile us to God, and God to us? By being a *propitiation*, ending judicial wrath against us. (See Rom. 3:24.)" He continues: "And how did the cross actually propitiate God? By being an event of *substitution*, whereby at the Father's will the sinless Son bore the retribution due to us guilty ones. (See 2 Cor. 5:21; Gal. 3:13; Col. 2:14.)"[7] Before I take a step back from this breathtaking set of altogether orthodox evangelical and Reformed claims, which he connects to all truly faithful believers and whose denial gets indirectly connected to heresy, I want to affirm that I believe in double imputation and that the word *propitiation* needs to have a place in our atonement theories, and therefore the concept of God's "wrath" must be factored in. So far so good, and mostly Reformed.

But let me push back for a more chastened biblical approach. First, double imputation is not clearly taught anywhere. I am restating Carson's own "unambiguously" and this must be added: even if imputational theology is implicit, and I think it is, one cannot lift something from the unambiguous-but-implicit level to front and center and sustain a sound biblical focus. There must be a reason why those earliest Christians never said anything quite like double imputation. Second, the weight placed for many on both "double imputation" and "propitiation" outstrips the biblical authors' own emphases. This follows from two facts, the first one being the "unambiguously" of Carson and the second one from this observation about Packer's famous study: the New Testament barely uses *pro-*

pitiation in the sense of God's wrath being poured out on Christ in order to vent the Father's just punishment against sin. Some, in fact, deny this idea can even be found in the New Testament. It is well known today that Romans 3:25, the only such reference in all of Paul, may mean "mercy seat" instead of "propitiation" (as it may also in Heb. 9:5). It is likely that the term means "propitiation" in 1 John 2:2.[8] Third, there is something nonevangelical about shaping one's theology on the basis of rare and questionable uses of terms in the New Testament, relying instead on logic, lifting such to central stage, and grounding one's theory more in the profound medieval and Reformation explanations of atonement than in the explicit and (less explicit) terms in the New Testament. In short, I find the narrowing of atonement to penal substitution, double imputation, and propitiation to be the result of an unfortunate zeal to protect Reformed theology instead of believing what the New Testament explicitly teaches. *Sola scriptura*, the reforming principle of the Reformation, does not permit the exaggeration that both double imputation and propitiation have been given in (neo-)Reformed theological circles.[9] Why not just let the New Testament say what it says? And that means we need to ask, what does it say?

We Have to Start in the Right Places

The narrowing of the gospel and atonement down to the central logical factors of both double imputation as the means of justification and propitiation—although the logic for each is both clear and compelling even if not central—begins with two major factors: God's utter holiness and humans' utter sinfulness. The ontological repulse of God to human sin is wrath, and there you have all that is needed for the current emphasis in many contemporary evangelical circles. Again, let me be clear: each of these elements must be factored in, but what is the price we are paying today for the virtual eradication and elimination of other biblically important and exegetically more central factors? I will put it this way: I am reasonably suspicious that it is our gospeling and evangelizing that have turned holiness, wrath, propitiation, and double imputation into the heart of the gospel.

That is, this stuff, when mixed into the proper brew of a compelling preacher and evangelist—like Billy Graham in his early days—is the heart of how to make the gospel sing and sting with sinners. Preach their sin, God's holiness and wrath, and God's gracious propitiation of his wrath in the cross of Christ, and you've got the gospel many preach. Again, let me be clear: each of these elements can be present in gospel preaching. But something has gone wrong, and I propose in this chapter to examine a few New Testament texts that reveal that the centralization of double imputation and propitiation blurs our ability to see what *gospel* means.

I want to put my cards on the table early so everyone will understand my argument. First, the centralization of double imputation and propitiation—and, once again, good, sound theological words—leads to a re-presentation of the gospel through those lenses.[10] Second, the more central these terms become in gospel theology, the less contact we have with the central gospel texts of the New Testament. Both points again: in essence, when double imputation and propitiation are elevated, gospel preaching involves the framing of our problem as guilt and being under the wrath of God. This leads to the presentation of Christ's death (rarely does resurrection emerge in this framing of the gospel) as the event whereby God's wrath is appeased (propitiation) and our guilt removed, and that removal by way of Christ assuming our sin and its penalty and our being graced with Christ's own perfect righteousness. Thus—and this is critically important for perceiving the issues at work in much of the gospel and atonement debates today—the central focus of the gospeler is to persuade humans to admit their fake and false righteousness and to accept the righteousness that alone is found in Christ's righteousness. Or, and this might be more common, the gospeler preaches in order to get humans to comprehend their dire situation of being under God's awful wrath, to feel the pangs of sin and sinfulness, and to cry out to God by clinging to Christ as the one who alone has absorbed God's wrath and to find in him the complete assuaging of God's wrath and the pacification of God in Christ. The two operative words are *reconciled* (peace with God) and *forgiven* (guilt removed through justification by way of double imputation). Atonement theories are driving the meaning of gospel.

My first contention is that this way of framing things is dialectical: gospel preaching and experiencing God's grace lead theologians to see justification, double imputation, and propitiation as central, and those terms have led gospelers to preach the gospel through those terms. Before long these terms are the lenses through which we see, and thus determine what we see.

My second contention is that the "gospeling" of the New Testament is not done this way. This is a bold claim, but it must be made: a faithful reading of the New Testament reveals that the "gospel" is not framed through the lenses of justification via double imputation or through the lens of propitiation. They are factors in how salvation was articulated by the apostles, but gospel preaching did not "tell that story." It told another one, and it was left to the earliest Christian theologians to articulate *how* salvation occurred, and that is just what atonement theories attempt to unravel. Justification and propitiation are entailments of the gospel, but they are not the driving forces. I shall attempt to prove this by focusing on one set of texts. In the book of Acts we find seven gospel sermons, and in these we see the two major apostles—Peter and then Paul—"evangelize" or "gospel" the gospel to their contemporaries. Those texts are Peter's in Acts 2:14–39; 3:12–25; 4:8–12; 10:34–43; and 11:5–18 and then Paul's in 13:16–41; 14:15–17; and 17:22–31.

Gospel, Atonement Theory, and the Book of Acts

I have been reading and teaching the book of Acts for most of my adult life, though I cannot be considered a specialist of Acts. For most of those years I have *assumed* and therefore *read into* the gospel sermons of Acts a fairly standard evangelical gospel, not unlike that given in the previous pages. But frustration recently led me to give this issue a fresh look, and what I found shocked me and led me to see other instances of "gospel" in that same fresh light. I cannot discuss those other texts in this setting, so I will restrict my observations to the book of Acts.

First, in the history of the church there have been a number of what is now called "atonement theories." These are defined and discussed in any good theology text, and you can also find them on Wikipedia: ransom, recapitulation, substitutionary, satisfaction, penal substitution, exemplary, and governmental. We can add to these some recent reframings, including the nonviolent atonement theory, which trades on the exemplary theory, and the Girardian theory of unmasking the powers at the cross where God takes the side of the victim and eschews any further appeal to scapegoat and violence. To complicate matters, one further thought must be constantly within our grasp: *the gospel itself is framed in the church through the lens of atonement theory*, and each of the atonement theories named above creates its own "gospel message." Thus, penal substitution theory begins with God's holiness and wrath and God's simultaneous love and grace and puts before the sinner the call to invoke the mercy of God in Christ's saving death. It would take pages to define each of these and the gospel that flows from them, but that is not my intent here. My point here is that *none of these atonement theories is at work in any central manner in the gospel preaching of the book of Acts*. Something else is at work.

Second, I want to reframe the first point in order to emphasize its significance by generalizing: *the gospel preaching events of the book of Acts are not driven by an atonement theory at all*. You can read Acts 2, 3, 4, 10, 11, 13, 14, and 17 and read atonement theory into the text, but an honest reading of those texts reveals that the gospel that Peter and Paul preached was not shaped by an atonement theory. They don't begin with our guilt or our inadequate righteousness or our standing under God's wrath or our need for God's grace or God's love or anything similar. They don't then move into the death of Christ as that which resolves *those* problems. Yes, by the time they are done preaching, such problems occasionally emerge, but something other than atonement theory was driving their gospel preaching.

This assertion is critical enough of what we are doing today that I need to clarify the implications. I'm not saying that gospel preaching shaped by justification or propitiation is wrong, nor am I suggesting that salvation is not intimately tied to these categories (though there are also many more). What I am saying is that we have reframed the gospel through the lens of atonement theory, and we have done so for a laundry list of reasons, not the least of which is the Reformation's (much-needed and I believe God-revived) refocusing of the creed through the lens of soteriology. Third, this is evident if one compares the Apostles' Creed or the Nicene Creed with either the Augsburg Confession or the Genevan Confession. There one finds an essentially trinitarian framework ("We believe in God the Father, God the Son, God the Spirit") reshaped in the Reformation confessions by a soteriological scheme. Thus, the Augsburg Confession begins with God and then moves to original sin, the Son of God, justification, the office of ministry, and then on to other topics. This Reformation insight, I suggest, led to a new lens through which we have learned to see the Bible and especially the "gospel." This lens is an atonement theory lens. It shapes everything evangelicalism believes.

My contention is not that this was wrong but rather that the Reformation created a "salvation" culture instead of a "gospel" culture, and in the process we have lost central features of the meaning of *gospel* and reshaped everything, including gospel, through the lens of soteriology. As a result, *gospel* now means "plan of salvation." The plan of salvation, I am also suggesting, is an entailment of the gospel, an articulation of how it happens, but the gospel itself was not originally the plan of salvation.

Now back to the book of Acts. Fourth, the basic narrative shape of the gospeling events by Peter and Paul, very much unlike most of our gospeling today, is *the Old Testament story coming to its fulfillment in the story of Jesus.* I know of no gospel tract today that even suggests that the problems in the story of Israel are what the gospel solves. Each of the gospel sermons in Acts illustrates this, but I'll focus on Acts 2, Peter's famous Pentecost "gospel" sermon. Peter begins with the accusation that the followers of Jesus were drunk and reveals that they are in fact filled with the Spirit, which filling fulfills Joel 2:28–32. This gives him the opportunity to speak about Jesus—his life, miracles, unjust accusation and death sentence, crucifixion, and God's raising him from the dead. This, in turn, gives him the opportunity to connect to the Old Testament Scriptures again, this time finding in David's words (Ps. 16:8–11) a glimpse of the resurrection. David, in fact, gives us more than a glimpse: David was to have a successor on the throne, and Jesus is just that person. God has not only raised him but exalted him to the right hand of God. This leads Peter to say that from that exalted position Jesus has sent the Spirit upon these followers of Jesus. And this prompts Peter to compare David to Jesus and show that Jesus was even more than David, for David anticipated Jesus's exaltation in Psalm 110:1. In light of Israel's story now being shown to come to its climactic fulfillment in Jesus's story, Peter calls his audience to "repent, and be baptized every one of you in the name of Jesus Christ so that your sins may be forgiven" (Acts 2:38). If they do, they too will receive the Holy Spirit, and Peter anchors that promise in Old Testament (though not citing a text) expectation (Acts 2:39).

The "gospel" sermon of Peter, which more or less represents the other gospel sermons in Acts, is driven by Israel's story finding its conclusive chapter in Jesus's story rather than by either an atonement theory or a personal salvation story. Atonement could be attributed to the sermon when Peter speaks of Jesus's being handed over and nailed to the cross (Acts 2:23), but it would have to be attributed to the text. Peter does not explain *how* that death accomplished anything. At any rate, one would have to add anything about justification, double imputation, and propitiation. Again, what drives the sermon is the Old Testament story finding its solution in Jesus's story.

Fifth, just to make this point clear, I present here the statements about the death of Jesus in the gospel sermons in Acts so that we have before us their descriptions of that death. There is barely a whiff of "how" Jesus's death was atonement: Jesus brings forgiveness and justification, but there is no direct connection of his death to either. These sermons mostly emphasize an unjust death that God overturned through resurrection. The point needs to be made: atonement theory does not drive this gospel preaching.

> This man, handed over to you according to the definite plan and fore-knowledge of God, you crucified and killed by the hands of those outside the law. But God raised him up, having freed him from death, because it was impossible for him to be held in its power. (2:23–24; cf. v. 38, forgiveness following repentance and baptism)

> The God of Abraham, the God of Isaac, and the God of Jacob, the God of our ancestors has glorified his servant Jesus, whom you handed over and rejected in the presence of Pilate, though he had decided to

release him. But you rejected the Holy and Righteous One and asked to have a murderer given to you, and you killed the Author of life, whom God raised from the dead. To this we are witnesses. . . . In this way God fulfilled what he had foretold through all the prophets, that his Messiah would suffer. (3:13–15, 18)

Let it be known to all of you, and to all the people of Israel, that this man is standing before you in good health by the name of Jesus Christ of Nazareth, whom you crucified, whom God raised from the dead. This Jesus is

> "the stone that was rejected by you, the builders;
>   it has become the cornerstone."

There is salvation in no one else, for there is no other name under heaven given among mortals by which we must be saved. (4:10–12)

We are witnesses to all that he did both in Judea and in Jerusalem. They put him to death by hanging him on a tree; but God raised him on the third day and allowed him to appear. (10:39–40; cf. v. 43, belief leads to forgiveness in his name)

Because the residents of Jerusalem and their leaders did not recognize him or understand the words of the prophets that are read every sabbath, they fulfilled those words by condemning him. Even though they found no cause for a sentence of death, they asked Pilate to have him killed. When they had carried out everything that was written about him, they took him down from the tree and laid him in a tomb. But God raised him from the dead. (13:27–30; cf. vv. 38–39, forgiveness and justification through Christ)

Sixth, unlike the emphasis in much of contemporary gospel preaching, which again is driven by an atonement theory, where we find a heavy, if not exclusive focus on the cross, the gospel sermons of Acts are one-sidedly focused on the *resurrection*. A notable statement, again from Peter but in Acts 3:15, is this: "You killed the Author of life, whom God raised from the dead." And Paul points to Jesus's resurrection as the singular act as well. From Acts 13:32–33: "What God promised our fathers he has fulfilled for us, their children, by raising up Jesus [from the dead]" (NIV). I emphasize this focus on resurrection because it was at the core of gospel preaching in Acts and it is nearly absent in any gospel preaching today. Leaving the discussion of the gospel sermons, where I've illustrated the resurrection in those events, let us now turn to the rest of the book of Acts. On trial before Felix, Paul sums up his message: "It is concerning the resurrection of the dead that I am on trial before you today" (24:21 NIV). Later, when Paul is before Festus, Festus lays the case quickly before King Agrippa with these words: "Instead, they [Paul's Jewish opponents] had some points of dispute with him about their own religion and about a dead man named Jesus who Paul claimed was alive" (25:19 NIV). When Paul stands before Agrippa, he says: "And now it is because of my hope [resurrection hope] in what God has promised our fathers that I am on trial today. . . . Why should any of you consider it incredible that God raises the dead?" (26:6, 8 NIV). And when Luke sums up Paul's preaching in Rome, in the last scene of Acts, he speaks again of the "hope of Israel" and his attempt to convince the Jews that Jesus is the one long hoped for in Israel's Scriptures and story (28:20, 23).

Seventh, in contrast to much of modern gospeling, which focuses emphatically on one's personal problem of sin and one's personal Savior and one's need of a personal decision—in other words, on *me, me, me*—all seven of the first gospeling events *focus emphatically on Jesus*. This is the point at which we have to make a choice on the path we are to travel, and I would like to make this not a false dichotomy but instead one of biblical emphasis. Contemporary gospeling focuses on personal decision and runs everything through the lens of atonement theory, while Peter's and Paul's sermons focus on Jesus and run everything through the lens of Israel's story. When we read Acts 2, 3, 4, 10, 11, 13, 14, and 17, we come away with Israel's grand narrative, which now finds its completion in Jesus's own story, and that story, somehow, brings forgiveness of sins and justification. In other words, the gospeling of Peter and Paul was the telling of the story of Jesus. Nothing says this better than Acts 10:36–38, which I will now quote in its entirety because it is one of the finest summaries of the gospel ever given. First Peter prepares his (mostly Gentile) audience for what he's going to tell them:

You know the message [*ton logon*] God sent to the people of Israel, telling the good news of peace through Jesus Christ, who is Lord of all. (NIV)

Then he fills in the lines of the gospel with these words:

You know what has happened throughout Judea, beginning in Galilee after the baptism that John preached—how God anointed Jesus of Nazareth with the Holy Spirit and power, and how he went around doing good and healing all who were under the power of the devil, because God was with him. (NIV)

Peter's words sketch the story of Jesus, which will then be filled out by telling of his death and resurrection and exaltation. What we need to recognize, however, is that for Peter *the story of Jesus is the gospel story*.

We need to pause for some reflection. Instead of the "gospel" being seen front and center as the "plan of salvation" or our personal salvation message that Jesus accomplishes for us, the apostolic gospel, it seems to me, was a story about Jesus that entailed a saving story in which we find forgiveness of sins and justification (cf. Acts 13:38–39). The order impresses me: tell the story of Jesus because that story saves. The concentration and one-sided focus on Jesus is worthy of more serious attention in gospel preaching today. Perhaps I need to emphasize this again: I urge you to read these gospel sermons to see for yourself. These are gospeling events, and they tell the gospel. What do you notice about the gospel in these sermons? One point will surely be apparent as you seek to answer that question: to gospel was to tell the story of Jesus as the climax of Israel's story.

Eighth, the gospeling of Peter and Paul in Acts is a species of declarative rhetoric instead of a highly individualized persuasive rhetoric. And what is declared or announced or "gospeled" is that Jesus, the one who was killed unjustly on the cross, was raised from the dead and was exalted to the right hand of God. This entire line of thinking is headed in one direction: the exalted one, Jesus, is *Messiah of Israel and Lord of all*.

Therefore let the entire house of Israel know with certainty that God has made him both Lord and Messiah, this Jesus whom you crucified. (Acts 2:36)

Fundamental to the earliest gospel is the announcement that Jesus, the one crucified and raised, is the Lord and the Messiah. To gospel is to announce his lordship.[11]

As we read the sermons in the book of Acts, one thing stands out that contrasts markedly with what we call evangelism today. Instead of beginning with our need or our problem, and making that problem more complex by connecting it to God's utter holiness, and then resolving that tension by appealing to Jesus's death on the cross as either a justifying act or a propitiating act, and then completing the rhetoric by appealing for a decision—instead of doing these things, the gospeling of Peter and Paul begins with the story of Israel and guides it to the specific events in the life of Jesus. The story was in search of a resolution and that came in the story of Jesus. This is all a species of *declarative rhetoric*. Peter's gospel announces and tells, and so does Paul's. Only after the announcement does Peter or Paul say "repent" or "believe" or "be baptized." In fact, the outsider might indeed ask why one needed to "repent." The rhetoric is declarative and only as a result of telling the story of Jesus does the gospeler tell others how to respond. The response desired, in other words, doesn't lead to a repackaging of how to tell the story.

Gospel Culture Recaptured

I mentioned earlier that the Reformation, for all its good, has led to a "salvation" culture instead of a "gospel" culture. This has created a profound problem for evangelicals: we are constantly trying to show the connection of salvation to transformation. So we try to show that justification inevitably leads to sanctification, or that justification leads to justice, or that regeneration leads to mobilization. I understand this impulse, but I would like to suggest that the near-reduction of "gospel" to "personal salvation" is at the heart of this problem, and recapturing the biblical sense of "gospel" will lead in an entirely different direction. Instead of persuading for personal salvation and then trying to connect people to the story of Jesus, we might begin with the story of Jesus and summon people to personal redemption by connecting to that story. I believe the emerging movement is struggling with this issue because of its robust commitment to the kingdom story of Jesus.

To put this struggle now in bolder terms, "justification" no more leads to justice than "regeneration" leads to mobilization, not because the latter don't matter—indeed they do immensely—but because we are trapped in one category and doing our best to jump from one category to the other. Justification leads to a verdict by God that we are in the right, and we can leave out for the moment all the recent debates about the new, the old, and fresh perspectives. Justification isn't designed to lead to justice as if it were automatic; it's a theological category with a narrower focus. Yes, I do agree that the justified should be just, and no one can completely separate the two, but the struggle to make the two more intimate has not been successful. And regeneration leads to new life, but asking it to speak to transformed morals is asking it to do too much. Regeneration undoes the problem of death. That's what it's designed to do. Yes, once again, all the qualifications can be included, but I contend that we are asking terms to do things they were not designed to do.

I believe one of the problems is that we have turned "gospel" into the "plan of salvation" and once we do that we lose connection to the breadth and expanse of "gospel." So I'd like to make this suggestion: *to gospel is to tell the story that Jesus is Lord and that we are to repent and believe and get baptized to enter into that lordship story.* The plan of salvation approach, I am suggesting, *only articulates how salvation occurs within that story and is not as expansive and broad as the gospel story.* The plan of salvation without the gospel can undercut the gospel, while the gospel leads to the plan of salvation every time.

By reducing gospel to plan of salvation, we have created a problem for which we now have very little rhetoric. That is, by reducing gospel to the plan of salvation, and by reducing the plan of salvation to a personal story of salvation, we sometimes have lost the gospel itself. But if we are to regain the fullness of the biblical gospel, which is the story of Israel finding its resolution in the Jesus story, and announcing that Jesus is Messiah and Lord over all, then we will have a story that leads inevitably to his lordship and discipleship, obedience, justice, and love. But if we continue to reduce gospel to salvation, seen through the lens of atonement theories, we will continue to struggle with the fact that the Jesus who is Savior is the Jesus who is Lord and Messiah.

Nothing illustrates this gospel versus salvation culture more than what one sees as the *problem* that the gospel seeks to solve. Clearly, the problem for justification is guilt; the problem for propitiation is the wrath of God; the problem for reconciliation is enmity; and the problem for redemption is enslavement. We could go on, but the logic of how this understanding works is eminently clear. Gospel preaching today often works through one of these problems. But what was the "gospel" preaching of Peter and Paul trying to solve? I want to lay out a few options, and when we "add" these to our typical "plan of salvation" gospel preaching, we gain a fullness and reclaim our whole New Testament. Indeed, we regain the story of the Bible. First, since the solution is resurrection, the problem is death. Second, since the solution is Jesus exalted as Messiah, the problem is the need for a true Davidic King to reign forever and ever. I wonder if we need to consider this issue more deeply than we have. Third, since the solution is the lordship of Jesus, the problem is the need to have a Lord and Master and our problem of being rebellious and in need of a Lord, or more: our problem is that God's people need to follow their Lord. Fourth, since the solution is the answer to Israel's story, we need to comprehend the story of Israel. So, here's a go at it: God made Adam and Eve to govern this world, but they chose not to and were exiled from Eden. Israel was appointed to be "priests and rulers" in this world and to be a blessing for the nations, but Israel failed, so God sent the One True Israelite, Jesus as Messiah, who is both Priest and King. This means that the solution to Israel's (in-search-of-a-solution) story is Jesus as Messiah, and thus the problem is that we are not governing the world as we ought. Jesus is that Governor; we are his vice-regents.

In short, Israel's story longs for a kingdom where God is King and where Israel is God's people in that kingdom. This, I submit to you, is exactly who Jesus is—Governor of heaven and earth—and exactly what Jesus preached: the kingdom of God. And this is what Paul was preaching in Acts 28. Personal salvation is what happens to people who enter into that story. The gospel is to tell that story aloud and point people to Jesus Christ as the Messiah and Lord.

Notes

Chapter 1 Who's Afraid of Philosophical Realism?

1. Bernard McGinn, *The Presence of God: A History of Western Christian Mysticism*, vol. 4, *The Harvest of Mysticism in Medieval Germany* (New York: Crossroad, 2005), 142.

2. Brian D. McLaren, *A New Kind of Christian: A Tale of Two Friends on a Spiritual Journey* (San Francisco: Jossey-Bass, 2001).

3. Tony Jones, *The New Christians: Dispatches from the Emergent Frontier* (San Francisco: Jossey-Bass, 2008).

4. Stanley Grenz, *A Primer on Postmodernism* (Grand Rapids: Eerdmans, 1996).

5. Robert Webber, *The Divine Embrace: Recovering the Passionate Spiritual Life* (Grand Rapids: Baker Books, 2006), 17.

6. Spencer Burke, *Heretics Guide to Eternity* (San Francisco: Jossey-Bass, 2006).

7. Peter Rollins, *How (Not) to Speak of God* (Brewster, MA: Paraclete Press, 2006).

8. Stanley Hauerwas, "Discipleship as a Craft: Church as a Disciplined Community," *Christian Century*, October 1, 1991, http://www.religion-online.org/showarticle .asp?title=110 (accessed January 2008).

9. Ibid.

10. Webber, *Divine Embrace*, 17.

Chapter 2 The Worldly Theology of Emerging Christianity

1. This definition does not limit such an entity to some intelligent, sentient being, for we can take such a definition to include the evocation of ideas such as nature, historical necessity, or destiny.

2. For the classic exposition of onto-theo-logy, see Martin Heidegger, "The Onto-theo-logical Constitution of Metaphysics," in *The Religious*, ed. John D. Caputo (Oxford: Blackwell, 2001), 67–75.

3. Dietrich Bonhoeffer, *Letters and Papers from Prison*, new and greatly enlarged ed. (New York: Touchstone, 1997), 281–82.

4. Martin Heidegger, "The Word of Nietzsche: 'God Is Dead,'" in *The Question Concerning Technology, and Other Essays*, trans. William Lovitt (London: Harper and Row, 1977), 63.

5. Ibid., 64.

6. These six conceptual phases closely resemble the four phases Jean Baudrillard writes of in *Simulacra and Simulation*, trans. Sheila Faria Glaser (Ann Arbor: University of Michigan Press, 2000), 6.

7. Friedrich Nietzsche, *Twilight of the Idols/The Anti-Christ*, trans. R. J. Hollingdale (London: Penguin, 1968), 40–41.

8. Graham Ward, "Introduction, or, A Guide to Theological Thinking in Cyberspace," in *The Postmodern God: A Theological Reader*, ed. Graham Ward (Oxford: Blackwell, 2001), xxviii.

9. Martin Heidegger, *Identity and Difference*, trans. Joan Stambaugh (New York: Harper and Row, 1969), 30.

10. Heidegger, "Onto-theo-logical Constitution of Metaphysics," 74.

11. Ibid., 68.

12. Dietrich Bonhoeffer, *Dietrich Bonhoeffer: Witness to Jesus Christ*, ed. John DeGruchy (London: Collins, 1988), 278.

13. Ibid., 291.

14. Ibid., 294.

Chapter 3 Consumer Liturgies and Their Corrosive Effects on Christian Identity

1. Sampling numbers of local churches and congregations, we estimate that less than 2 percent of our local community is connected to a church in any form.

2. For a book that explains this process in detail, see Vincent Jude Miller's *Consuming Religion: Christian Faith and Practice in a Consumer Culture* (New York: Continuum, 2003).

3. Ibid., 90.

4. Ibid., 84.

5. For an example of how human identity is shaped by the market rather than by religious faith in a post-Protestant work-ethic world, see Peter H. Sedgwick, *The Market Economy and Christian Ethics*, New Studies in Christian Ethics (Cambridge: Cambridge University Press, 1999).

6. Miller, *Consuming Religion*, 29.

7. Ibid., 85.

8. Oliver O'Donovan, *Resurrection and Moral Order: An Outline for Evangelical Ethics*, 2nd ed. (Leicester, UK: Apollos, 1994), 230.

9. This is the question posed and explored in Simon Chan, "The Ontology of the Church," in *Liturgical Theology: The Church as Worshiping Community* (Downers Grove, IL: InterVarsity, 2006), 21–40.

10. Michael Frost and Alan Hirsch, *The Shaping of Things to Come: Innovation and Mission for the 21st Century Church* (Peabody, MA: Hendrickson, 2003), 209.

11. Ibid.

12. For a most comprehensive description and understanding of the church in that way, see Oliver O'Donovan, *The Desire of the Nations: Rediscovering the Roots of Political Theology* (Cambridge: Cambridge University Press, 1996).

13. Chan, "Ontology of the Church," 24.

14. Luke Bretherton, "A Proposal for How Christians and Non-Christians Should Relate to Each Other with Regards to Ethical Disputes in Light of Alasdair Macintyre, Germain Grisez and Oliver O'Donovan's Work" (PhD diss., King's College London, 2001), 161.

15. I've taken the phrase "blueprint ecclesiologies" from Nicholas M. Healy, *Church, World and the Christian Life: Practical-Prophetic Ecclesiology* (Cambridge: Cambridge University Press, 2000).

16. If I may paraphrase badly Alasdair C. MacIntyre, *After Virtue: A Study in Moral Theory* (London: Duckworth, 1981).

17. Luke Bretherton makes this clear in his chapter "Beyond the Emerging Church," in *Remembering Our Future: Explorations in Deep Church*, ed. Andrew Walker and Luke Bretherton (Milton Keynes, UK: Paternoster, 2007), 38.

18. Ibid.

19. For an early description of "third space," see Ray Oldenburg, "The Character of Third Places," in *The Great Good Place: Cafés, Coffee Shops, Community Centers, Beauty Parlors, General Stores, Bars, Hangouts, and How They Get You through the Day* (New York: Paragon, 1989), 20–42.

20. Ori Brafman and Rod A. Beckstrom, *The Starfish and the Spider: The Unstoppable Power of Leaderless Organizations* (New York: Portfolio, 2006).

21. Ibid., 194.

22. This "canonical-linguistic" turn is something suggested in Kevin J. Vanhoozer, *The Drama of Doctrine: A Canonical-Linguistic Approach to Christian Theology* (Louisville: Westminster John Knox, 2005).

23. A process ably described by Brian D. McLaren, *The Story We Find Ourselves In: Further Adventures of a New Kind of Christian* (San Francisco: Jossey-Bass, 2003).

24. For a description of this process, see Reinhard Hütter, *Suffering Divine Things: Theology as Church Practice*, trans. Doug Stott (Grand Rapids: Eerdmans, 2000), 191.

25. Joseph Heath and Andrew Potter, *The Rebel Sell: How the Counterculture Became Consumer Culture* (Chichester, UK: Capstone, 2006).

26. Eric Gregory, *Politics and the Order of Love: An Augustinian Ethic of Democratic Citizenship* (Chicago: University of Chicago Press, 2008), 286.

27. Immanuel Kant, *Lectures on Anthropology*, 25.592.

28. Spencer Burke, "Spencer Burke on the Church That Consumerism Built—and Why I Fled," Out of Ur Blog, posted May 3, 2006, http://www.outofur.com/archives/2006/05/spencer_burke_o_1.html (accessed June 26, 2009).

29. Chan, "Ontology of the Church," 36.

30. Hütter, *Suffering Divine Things*, 192.

Chapter 4 Thy Kingdom Come (on Earth)

1. "You've Been Left Behind," lyrics by Larry Norman.

2. "Grand Rapids, MI: Excerpts from a 24-7 Community," http://www.24-7prayer .us/content/view/47/119/1/3/images/index.php?option=com_content&task=view&id =119&Itemid=114&PHPSESSID=52465e850e63bae866c14fb58eaa2a7b (accessed September 3, 2010).

Chapter 5 The Renewal of Liturgy in the Emerging Church

1. For examples of how evangelicals are retrieving liturgy and traditions, see D. H. Williams, *Retrieving the Tradition and Renewing Evangelicalism: A Primer for Suspicious Protestants* (Grand Rapids: Eerdmans, 1999); and Mark Galli, *Beyond Smells and Bells: The Wonder and Power of Christian Liturgy* (Brewster, MA: Paraclete, 2008).

2. My church is part of The Association of Vineyard Churches UK.

3. Emine Saner, "Sick on Arrival," *Guardian*, July 31, 2007, http://www.guardian.co.uk/lifeandstyle/2007/jul/31/healthandwellbeing.health#article (accessed December 22, 2007).

4. Theos News, "Only 1 in 8 People Know the Christmas Story Well," *Theos: The Public Theology Think Tank*, December 8, 2007, http://www.theosthinktank.co.uk/Only_1_in_8_people_know_the_Christmas_Story_well.aspx?ArticleID=1411&PageID=14&RefPageID=5 (December 2008).

5. Walter Brueggemann, *Biblical Perspectives on Evangelism: Living in a Three-Storied Universe* (Nashville: Abingdon, 1993). Andrew Walker has developed this notion in his *Telling the Story: Gospel, Mission and Culture*, Gospel and Culture (London: SPCK, 1996).

6. Brian D. McLaren, *The Story We Find Ourselves In: Further Adventures of a New Kind of Christian*. San Francisco: Jossey-Bass, 2003. See also his *A New Kind of Christian: A Tale of Two Friends on a Spiritual Journey* (San Francisco: Jossey-Bass, 2001).

7. For an explanation of the nature of the Church Calendar see Luke Bretherton, "Mundane Holiness: The Theology and Spirituality of Everyday Life," in *Remembering Our Future: Explorations in Deep Church*, ed. Andrew Walker and Luke Bretherton (Milton Keynes, UK: Paternoster, 2007), 236.

8. Vincent Jude Miller, *Consuming Religion: Christian Faith and Practice in a Consumer Culture* (New York: Continuum, 2003), 90.

9. Alain De Botton, *Status Anxiety* (London: Hamish Hamilton, 2004).

10. Bretherton, "Mundane Holiness," 241.

11. See http://flow.vineyardchurch.org.

Chapter 6 Transformance Art

1. Slavoj Žižek, *On Belief* (London: Routledge, 2001), 15.

2. Slavoj Žižek, *The Puppet and the Dwarf* (London: MIT Press, 2003), 26.

3. Karl Marx, "Contribution to the Critique of Hegel's Philosophy of Law" in *Karl Marx, Friedrich Engels: Collected Works*, ed. Maria Shcheglova, Tatyana Grishina, and Lyudgarda Zubdlova (London: Lawrence and Wishart, 1975), 3:176.

Chapter 7 Scripture in the Emerging Movement

1. I draw here from a chapter in my book *The Blue Parakeet: Rethinking How You Read the Bible* (Grand Rapids: Zondervan, 2008), 41–54, though I develop those thoughts anew in this new piece.

2. The exam can be found as appendix 2 in *The Blue Parakeet*, 220–23. The intent of the exam is to reveal that, if given to enough folks, a pattern will emerge: most people think Jesus has similar characteristics and attributes to the test-taker, regardless of the basic personality type. This reveals projection.

3. This raises the issue of canon and even canon criticism, which can't be dealt with in the context of this essay.

4. On postmodernity's linguistic focus, see Myron B. Penner, ed., *Christianity and the Postmodern Turn: Six Views* (Grand Rapids: Brazos, 2005); James K. A. Smith, *Who's Afraid of Postmodernism? Taking Derrida, Lyotard, and Foucault to Church*, The Church and Postmodern Culture (Grand Rapids: Baker Academic, 2006); John D. Caputo, *Philosophy and Theology* (Nashville: Abingdon, 2006). A particular application of this to God-talk is Peter Rollins, *How (Not) to Speak of God* (Brewster, MA: Paraclete, 2006); for application to hermeneutics, the seminal work is perhaps George A. Lindbeck, *The Nature of Doctrine: Religion and Theology in a Postliberal Age* (Louisville: Westminster John Knox, 1984); an evangelical form is found in Kevin J. Vanhoozer, *The Drama of Doctrine: A Canonical-Linguistic Approach to Christian Theology* (Louisville: Westminster John Knox, 2005).

5. Michael Fishbane, *Sacred Attunement: A Jewish Theology* (Chicago: University of Chicago Press, 2008); I draw here from 141–45.

6. Unless I'm mistaken, this allusion to the famous song ("How Great Thou Art") sung by George Beverly Shea at Billy Graham rallies from the late 1950s on illustrates one of Fishbane's scholarly themes: intertextuality.

7. Fishbane mentions this distinction of Torah in a few places in *Sacred Attunement*; see, e.g., 60–62.

8. John Goldingay, *Old Testament Theology*, vol. 1, *Israel's Gospel* (Downers Grove, IL: InterVarsity, 2003), 24.

Chapter 8 Atonement and Gospel

1. J. R. Woodward, ed., *ViralHope: Good News from the Urbs to the Burbs (and Everything in Between)* (Los Angeles: Ecclesia Press, 2010).

2. The papers from the conference can be found in Mark Husbands and Daniel J. Treier, eds., *Justification: What's at Stake in the Current Debates* (Downers Grove, IL: IVP Academic, 2004).

3. Scot McKnight, *Jesus and His Death: Historiography, the Historical Jesus, and Atonement Theory* (Waco: Baylor University Press, 2005).

4. Robert H. Gundry, "The Nonimputation of Christ's Righteousness," in *Justification: What's at Stake in the Current Debates*, ed. Mark Husbands and Daniel J. Treier (Downers Grove, IL: InterVarsity, 2004), 25.

5. D. A. Carson, "The Vindication of Imputation," in *Justification: What's at Stake in the Current Debates*, ed. Mark Husbands and Daniel J. Treier (Downers Grove, IL: InterVarsity, 2004), 46.

6. Ibid., 78.

7. J. I. Packer and Mark Dever, *In My Place Condemned He Stood* (Wheaton: Crossway, 2007), 25. This book republishes what I think is the finest statement ever on penal substitution by Packer; see 53–100. I read this piece in seminary, underlined and marked it up, and have returned to it routinely in my career. While Packer's piece lacks a classic evangelical exegetical approach—there are pages without reference to the Bible—I think he gets most things right.

8. There is a long-standing debate among evangelicals about this term, and it involves a debate between C. H. Dodd and L. L. Morris that need not be described here.

9. By "(neo-)Reformed" I mean the Alliance of Confessing Evangelicals, Together for the Gospel, and the Gospel Coalition organizations, led by such pillars as John Piper, D. A. Carson, David Wells, Al Mohler, and Mark Dever.

10. An excellent, nuanced statement to this effect can be found at the Gospel Coalition site: http://thegospelcoalition.org/about/foundation-documents/confessional/. It is more commonly found in less nuanced form in gospel tracts and in gospel preaching in local churches, coffee shops, and homes.

11. There is a host of good scholarship on this, but I mention G. N. Stanton, *Jesus and Gospel* (Cambridge: Cambridge University Press, 2004), esp. 9–62. Again, "to gospel" was in the ancient world "to herald" or "to declare" or "to announce" good news.

Bibliography

Berlin, Isaiah. "The Hedgehog and the Fox: An Essay on Tolstoy's View of History." In *The Proper Study of Mankind: An Anthology of Essays*, edited by Henry Hardy and Roger Hausheer, 436–98. New York: Farrar, Straus and Giroux, 2000.

Bonhoeffer, Dietrich. *Dietrich Bonhoeffer: Witness to Jesus Christ*. Edited by John DeGruchy. London: Collins, 1988.

Brafman, Ori, and Rod A. Beckstrom. *The Starfish and the Spider: The Unstoppable Power of Leaderless Organizations*. New York: Portfolio, 2006.

Brueggemann, Walter. *Biblical Perspectives on Evangelism: Living in a Three-Storied Universe*. Nashville: Abingdon, 1993.

Carson, D. A. "The Vindication of Imputation." In Husbands and Treier, *Justification*, 46–79. Downers Grove, IL: InterVarsity, 2004.

Chan, Simon. *Liturgical Theology: The Church as Worshiping Community*. Downers Grove, IL: InterVarsity, 2006.

De Botton, Alain. *Status Anxiety*. London: Hamish Hamilton, 2004.

Frost, Michael, and Alan Hirsch. *The Shaping of Things to Come: Innovation and Mission for the 21st Century Church*. Peabody, MA: Hendrickson, 2003.

Goldingay, John. *Old Testament Theology*. Vol. 1, *Israel's Gospel*. Downers Grove, IL: InterVarsity, 2003.

Gregory, Eric. *Politics and the Order of Love: An Augustinian Ethic of Democratic Citizenship*. Chicago: University of Chicago Press, 2008.

Gundry, Robert H. "The Nonimputation of Christ's Righteousness." In Husbands and Treier, *Justification*, 17–45.

Healy, Nicholas M. *Church, World and the Christian Life: Practical-Prophetic Ecclesiology*. Cambridge: Cambridge University Press, 2000.

Heath, Joseph, and Andrew Potter. *The Rebel Sell: How the Counterculture Became Consumer Culture*. Chichester, UK: Capstone, 2006.

Heidegger, Martin. *Identity and Difference*. Translated by Joan Stambaugh. New York: Harper and Row, 1969.

———. "The Onto-theo-logical Constitution of Metaphysics." In *The Religious*, edited by John D. Caputo, 67–75. Oxford: Blackwell, 2001.

———. "The Word of Nietzsche: 'God Is Dead.'" In *The Question Concerning Technology, and Other Essays*, translated by William Lovitt, 53–112. New York: Harper and Row, 1977.

Husbands, Mark, and Daniel J. Treier, eds. *Justification: What's at Stake in the Current Debates*. Downers Grove, IL: InterVarsity, 2004.

Hütter, Reinhard. *Suffering Divine Things: Theology as Church Practice*. Translated by Doug Stott. Grand Rapids: Eerdmans, 2000.

Kimball, Dan. *Emerging Worship: Creating Worship Gatherings for New Generations*. Grand Rapids: EmergentYS; Zondervan, 2004.

MacIntyre, Alasdair C. *After Virtue: A Study in Moral Theory*. London: Duckworth, 1981.

Marx, Karl, and Friedrich Engles. *Collected Works*. Vol. 3. Edited by Maria Shcheglova, Tatyana Grishina, and Lyudgarda Zubdlova. London: Lawrence and Wishart, 1975.

McGinn, Bernard. *The Presence of God: A History of Western Christian Mysticism*. Vol. 4, *The Harvest of Mysticism in Medieval Germany*. New York: Crossroad, 2005.

McKnight, Scot. *The Actuality of the Atonement*. Grand Rapids: Eerdmans, 1989.

———. *The Blue Parakeet: Rethinking How You Read the Bible*. Grand Rapids: Zondervan, 2008.

———. *Jesus and His Death: Historiography, the Historical Jesus, and Atonement Theory*. Waco: Baylor University Press, 2005.

McLaren, Brian D. *A New Kind of Christian: A Tale of Two Friends on a Spiritual Journey*. San Francisco: Jossey-Bass, 2001.

———. *The Story We Find Ourselves In: Further Adventures of a New Kind of Christian*. San Francisco: Jossey-Bass, 2003.

Miller, Vincent Jude. *Consuming Religion: Christian Faith and Practice in a Consumer Culture*. New York: Continuum, 2003.

Nietzsche, Friedrich. *Twilight of the Idols/The Anti-Christ*. Translated by R. J. Hollingdale. London: Penguin, 1968.

O'Donovan, Oliver. *The Desire of the Nations: Rediscovering the Roots of Political Theology*. Cambridge: Cambridge University Press, 1996.

———. *Resurrection and Moral Order: An Outline for Evangelical Ethics*. 2nd ed. Leicester, UK: Apollos, 1994.

Oldenburg, Ray. *The Great Good Place: Cafés, Coffee Shops, Community Centers, Beauty Parlors, General Stores, Bars, Hangouts and How They Get You through the Day*. New York: Paragon, 1989.

Packer, J. I., and Mark Dever. *In My Place Condemned He Stood*. Wheaton: Crossway, 2007.

Saner, Emine. "Sick on Arrival." *Guardian*, July 31, 2007. http://www.guardian.co.uk/lifeandstyle/2007/jul/31/healthandwellbeing.health#article (accessed December 22, 2007).

Sedgwick, Peter H. *The Market Economy and Christian Ethics*. New Studies in Christian Ethics. Cambridge: Cambridge University Press, 1999.

Stanton, G. N. *Jesus and Gospel*. Cambridge: Cambridge University Press, 2004.

Theos News. "Only 1 in 8 People Know the Christmas Story Well." *Theos: The Public Theology Think Tank*, December 8, 2007. http://www.theosthinktank.co.uk/Only_1_in_8_people_know_the_Christmas_Story_well.aspx?ArticleID=1411&PageID=14&RefPageID=5 (accessed December 22, 2007).

Vanhoozer, Kevin J. *The Drama of Doctrine: A Canonical-Linguistic Approach to Christian Theology*. Louisville: Westminster John Knox, 2005.

Walker, Andrew. *Telling the Story: Gospel, Mission and Culture*. Gospel and Culture. London: SPCK, 1996.

Walker, Andrew, and Luke Bretherton, eds. *Remembering Our Future*. Milton Keynes, UK: Paternoster, 2007.

Ward, Graham, ed. *The Postmodern God: A Theological Reader*. Oxford: Blackwell, 2001.

Webber, Robert. *Ancient-Future Faith: Rethinking Evangelicalism for a Postmodern World*. Grand Rapids: Baker Books, 1999.

Williams, D. H. *Retrieving the Tradition and Renewing Evangelicalism: A Primer for Suspicious Protestants*. Grand Rapids: Eerdmans, 1999.

Woodward, J. R., ed. *ViralHope: Good News from the Urbs to the Burbs (and Everything in Between)*. Los Angeles: Ecclesia Press, 2010.

Žižek, Slavoj. *On Belief*. London: Routledge, 2001.

———. *The Puppet and the Dwarf*. London: MIT Press, 2003.

Contributors

Jason Clark completed his doctor of ministry degree in theology and leadership from George Fox Seminary and is midway through a PhD program in theology at King's College London, where he is researching the nature of ecclesiology within capitalism and consumer contexts. He is a sought after speaker for conferences on faith and culture and leads a doctor of ministry program in Global Missional Leadership at George Fox Seminary in Washington.

Kevin Corcoran is professor of philosophy at Calvin College. Recognized as a gifted teacher and speaker, Corcoran has written or edited two books and authored many articles in the areas of philosophy of religion, metaphysics, and the philosophy of mind. Of late he has begun to write for wider, more popular audiences.

Scot McKnight, professor in religious studies at North Park University, is a widely recognized authority on the New Testament, early Christianity, and the historical Jesus. He is the author of more than thirty books, including *A Community Called Atonement* (Abingdon, 2007) and *James* in the New International Commentary (Eerdmans, 2010).

Belfast native **Peter Rollins** has been praised as one of the most provocative and thoughtful theologians of our day. An author, lecturer, and storyteller, he is renowned for his dynamic and winsome speaking. Rollins is also the founder of ikon, a faith group that has gained an international reputation for blending live music, visual imagery, soundscapes, theater, ritual, and reflection to create what they call "transformance art." Rollins received his PhD in post-structural thought from Queen's College, Belfast. He is currently a research associate with the Irish School of Ecumenics at Trinity College in Dublin and is the author of the groundbreaking book *How (Not) to Speak of God*. His most recent work is titled *The Orthodox Heretic and Other Impossible Tales*.

Index

153